THE COMMUNITY'S COLLEGE

THE COMMUNITY'S COLLEGE

The Pursuit of Democracy, Economic Development, and Success

Robert L. Pura and Tara L. Parker

Foreword by Lynn Pasquerella

STERLING, VIRGINIA

COPYRIGHT © 2022 BY AAC&U AND STYLUS PUBLISHING, LLC

Copublished by AAC&U and Stylus Publishing, LLC.

AAC&U
1818 R Street NW
Washington, DC 20009

Stylus Publishing, LLC
22883 Quicksilver Drive
Sterling, Virginia 20166-2019

Library of Congress Cataloging-in-Publication Data

Names: Pura, Robert L., author. | Parker, Tara L., author.
Title: The community's college : the pursuit of democracy, economic development, and success / Robert L. Pura and Tara L. Parker ; foreword by Lynn Pasquerella.
Description: First Edition. | Sterling, Virginia : Stylus Publishing, LLC, [2022] | Includes bibliographical references and index. | Summary: "As well as offering an important message to state and federal policy makers, this book serves as a roadmap for aspiring leaders of community colleges as well as a text for leadership and higher education courses"-- Provided by publisher.
Identifiers: LCCN 2022020414 (print) | LCCN 2022020415 (ebook) | ISBN 9781642674248 (Cloth : acid-free paper) | ISBN 9781642674255 (Paperback: acid-free paper) | ISBN 9781642674262 (Library networkable e-edition) | ISBN 9781642674279 (Consumer e-edition)
Subjects: LCSH: Community colleges--United States. | Community and college--United States. | Educational leadership--United States. | Higher education and state--United States.
Classification: LCC LB2328 .P87 2022 (print) | LCC LB2328 (ebook) | DDC 378.1/5430973--dc23/eng/20220609
LC record available at https://lccn.loc.gov/2022020414
LC ebook record available at https://lccn.loc.gov/2022020415

13-digit ISBN: 978-1-64267-424-8 (cloth)
13-digit ISBN: 978-1-64267-425-5 (paperback)
13-digit ISBN: 978-1-64267-426-2 (library networkable e-edition)
13-digit ISBN: 978-1-64267-427-9 (consumer e-edition)

Printed in the United States of America

All first editions printed on acid-free paper
that meets the American National Standards Institute
Z39-48 Standard.

Bulk Purchases

Quantity discounts are available for use in workshops and for staff development.

Call 1-800-232-0223

First Edition, 2022

For Marjorie and Mary,
my teachers and mentors,
and for
all who teach and learn in community colleges,
this book is yours.

—Bob Pura

For my daughter Nikki, who makes improbable dreams
possible.

—Tara Parker

CONTENTS

FOREWORD

In the months following the March 11, 2020, announcement by the World Health Organization of the emergence of a global pandemic, psychologists pointed to the growing phenomenon of people turning to nostalgia, with memories of happier times serving as a stabilizing force in response to loss, suffering, anxiety, isolation, and uncertainty. I confess that I was among those who began sifting through old albums and shoeboxes during long periods of lockdown, when gathering with friends and family to celebrate birthdays, graduations, weddings, and taking vacations became a distant memory. It was amid one of these sojourns into the past that I came across an unexpected find.

Newspaper clippings, letters, postcards, and photos piled in a large plastic bin were interspersed with grade reports, term papers, and bluebooks—part of an entire collection of ephemera from my first semester at Quinebaug Valley Community College in the fall of 1976. The college that launched my academic career had opened just 5 years earlier in the small, rural town in which I lived. At 17, I decided to forgo a full scholarship to attend my state's flagship university so I could stay home and serve as a caregiver for my mother, who was chronically ill. Quinebaug provided a lifeline, enabling me to meet my personal obligations while becoming the first in my family to attend college. Classes were held in familiar places of belonging—biology in the high school from which I graduated; philosophy and political science at St. James elementary, where I attended Catechism every Saturday from First Communion through confirmation; American literature in the basement of the Congregational Church, where I accompanied my mother three times a year to give blood; and the history of Russia and China at the Ellis Technical School, whose parking lot functioned as a training ground for my learning to drive a standard shift.

Though the venues were well known to me, the intellectual vitality to which I was exposed within their walls was something I had never experienced. As a result, the artifacts I chose to preserve were not only markers of time, but also clumsy attempts at curating a life by arranging and classifying bits and pieces of a world that was both new and exciting. Copies of financial aid forms; a work contract for 35 hours a week under funding from the Comprehensive Employment and Training Act; a notice of a Pell grant award; theater ticket stubs and chopsticks from the night my classmates and I traveled 50 miles to see a play at the Hartford Stage and discuss its themes over Chinese food; and stacks of bluebooks were physical manifestations of an effort at meaning-making during a moment of profound personal change.

So, it was fitting that the first bluebook I opened contained my answer from an essay exam on Aristotle's response to the philosophical problem of change. How is it possible for something to change and yet endure throughout? I used an entire booklet to address this first of four questions on Aristotelian metaphysics, meticulously detailing Aristotle's distinction between the form of individual substances—their actuality—and their matter, or potentiality. For Aristotle, change involves the actualizing of a potentiality of the subject, and it is the matter that remains while the form changes. At each successive stage, the old matter is actualized into a new form, yet leaves the potential for another new form to be actualized. The essay concludes with the explanation that "these individual substances exist in an ordered hierarchy. Each depending on the others. For each substance is both the form or actualization of its previous matter and at the same time the basis for other forms and actualizations." I did not understand then, as I do now, that this final paragraph of my response would serve as a metaphor for my own transformation—possibility actualized through a system of interdependent individuals, challenging me to explore life's big questions, empowering me to become an innovator in my own life, and providing me with the intellectual skills necessary to succeed.

The diverse narratives captured in *The Community's College* demonstrate the ways in which community colleges continue to serve as powerful catalysts for social and economic mobility, not only for the students whose stories are told here, but for their families and the communities in which they are located. Equally important, the analysis offered by Pura and Parker unveils how community colleges—distinctively American institutions—are more essential than ever to fulfilling our nation's historic mission of educating for democracy.

—Lynn Pasquerella
President, American Association of Colleges and Universities

ACKNOWLEDGMENTS

There are many we would like to acknowledge for encouraging this journey. We want to especially thank everyone at the Association of American Colleges and Universities (AAC&U): Lynn Pasqeurella and David Tritelli, your support and faith in this book brought it to life. AAC&U is indeed a voice and a force, educating for democracy. John von Knorring and Marianna Vertullo at Stylus Publishing individually and collectively guided *The Community's College* into a far better place.

Thank you Damita Davis for proofreading this book and for not giving up when computer software tried to prevent you from doing so.

To the leaders, faculty, staff, students, and communities of Connors State College, Hostos Community College, Grand Rapids Community College, Diné College, and Berkeley City College, we thank you for your time and your stories. You are creating the America we need.

Most especially, to all those who yearn to breathe free, you taught us why.

Bob would like to acknowledge the Greenfield Community College Trustees and Foundation Board, and his students, colleagues and friends at Massasoit, Berkshire, and Greenfield Community Colleges. Thank you all for every day of those 40 years. Your love and commitment to college and community has been inspirational.

It was halftime. Aspiring to lead and better serve the community college movement, I wanted to go into the locker room and learn from the best. I found the best in John and Suanne Roueche, George Baker, my professors and fellow blockers in CCLP at UT. "Powerful stuff," coach. Byron and Kay McClenney not only welcomed me to CCD with warmth and direction, but you included us as signing members of the bathroom wall club of friends and colleagues. You all taught me so much more than content.

My deep appreciation for all at AACC as well. From George Zook and Edmund Gleazer to George Boggs and Walter Bumphus, because of your leadership, passion, and commitment, a movement, to make good on the promises of our nation, was born and lives on.

To Barbara, Kaitlyn, Linda, Phyllis and Archie, Sir Lawrence, and especially Marje and Mary, thank you all for the sounding board and loving encouragement you gave me along the way.

Tara would like to acknowledge, Amy Collinsworth and Shantal Petrie for holding it down while I was away from the office working on this book. Cheryl Ching, an expert in equity and community colleges, was a great sounding board throughout the process. I also want to thank my students and alumni of the UMass Boston Higher Education Program, some of whom are cited in this book. Your work and dedication to creating change continues to inspire me.

Nothing in my life is possible without the love and support of my family. Mom, Dad, Heather, Scott, Jody, Daren, and Deb, you ground me. We lost Gertie along the way, and I appreciate the many hours she hung out with me while I wrote, usually asleep, at my feet or on my lap. Shaunya supported me throughout the writing of this book and everything else. Nikki, my daughter, made me laugh and made me dinner. I am grateful.

INTRODUCTION

Since the first independent, public two-year college (then known as a junior college) opened its doors in 1901, community colleges have been asked to do the impossible: promote American ideals of democracy, opportunity, and social mobility, at times when even our federal government turned its back on these principles. Indeed, the American creed of democracy has never held true for millions of Americans of African, Asian, Latin American, and/or Indigenous descent, the same populations that make up the majority of community college students. Further, community colleges enroll 41% of all undergraduates (American Association of Community Colleges [AACC], 2021) and nearly half (49%) of all students who go on to complete a four-year degree (Community College Research Center [CCRC], 2020). Despite the demands on and the diversity of community colleges, they remain the least resourced and the least funded institutions in the United States (AACC, 2021), calling our democracy and the purpose of our nation's community colleges into question.

Throughout this book, we seek to deepen awareness of the ways community colleges address these social and economic challenges by being responsive to their respective communities and seeking to live up to the promise of democracy. Specifically, we share stories from Bob Pura's lived experiences as a former president of a community college alongside his visits to five additional campuses from across the nation. Each chapter is followed by critical reflections offered by Tara Parker, whose higher education scholarship and leadership is grounded in racial and social justice. Together we address the need for college leaders who are committed to building community on and off campus and to advocating for those communities. We also consider community colleges' ability to respond to crises, whether they be global pandemics or chronic racial conflict, all with limited fiscal resources. The community colleges' responsibilities to develop a multiracial and diverse democracy and to develop the local workforce and economies while remaining accessible and affordable are central themes throughout. Given the significance of this educational sector, this book serves as a call to action of state policymakers to increase support for community colleges, as they are vital to our nation's future. At a time when policymakers and

1

the general public are increasingly concerned about college affordability, economic growth, and racial conflict, these considerations have never been more timely or relevant. We hope our readers will engage in these important conversations with us. In so doing, we expect students in higher education graduate programs, future and new college leaders, and policymakers will use this book, and the stories within it, as an opportunity to reflect and create change within and in support of community colleges in hopes of realizing our democracy.

Diverse Students, Diverse Mission

The mission of community colleges is as diverse as their students. Community colleges were founded and grew at a time when higher education institutions were becoming increasingly stratified. Indeed, as access to higher education expanded in the United States, particularly after World War II, it became more hierarchical. Thus, two-year institutions were founded on and developed amid a persistent debate on their purpose. Some advocated for two-year institutions to be an extension of high school where students would develop more technical skills and be prepared for semi-professional positions rather than professional ones. Others advocated for two-year colleges to serve as "junior colleges," preparing students for the four-year college or university and focusing on transfer courses and social mobility (Brint & Karabel, 1989b). These debates about the mission of community colleges are still visibly present today as their purpose has only expanded over the past 100 years.

While debates about transfer and vocationalization continue, some community colleges have added baccalaureate degrees to their credential offerings, raising more questions about their institutional purpose. At the same time, community colleges are expected to accept all who knock on their doors. In addition to supporting transfer for a bachelor's degree or preparing students for the labor market, two-year colleges train adult learners in basic education and lifelong learning programs. Their campuses are open to the communities in which they reside, offering job training and cultural programming and events to all. It is not surprising then, that community colleges reach so many individuals.

Nearly 12 million students take courses at community colleges for job training, increasing skills, or transfer toward a baccalaureate degree. Nearly seven million of these students are enrolled in credit-bearing courses, including 37% whose families earned less than $20,000 annually. The majority (59%) of community college students receive some type of financial aid, including

33% who receive Pell grants. Most community college students work full-time while going to school. Nearly a third of all community college students are the first in their families to attend college (AACC, 2021). Each year, half of all undergraduates of color enroll in community colleges. More than half of all Latinx and Native American undergraduate students (CCRC, 2020) and more than 40% of Black, Asian, and white undergraduates respectively enrolled in community colleges in fall 2018. In fall 2019, at least 52% of all community college students, enrolled for credit, were students of color (see Table I.1).

Community colleges also play an important role in the degree completion agenda as nearly half of all who graduate with a four-year degree once attended a community college. Most of these attended for at least three or more terms (CCRC, 2020). Additionally, most high schools partner with community colleges to offer dual enrollment courses (CCRC, 2020), allowing students to earn college credit while still in high school. At the same time, the majority of community college students are enrolled in at least one developmental education course, and too many never complete despite high aspirations. Thus, two-year institutions have a particular responsibility to reform, improve, and even reconsider developmental education with the goal of increasing course and degree completion for those students enrolled.

This is especially important as the nation grapples with several existential crises and major shifts in demographics. The U.S. population is aging, and growth is stagnant, due in part to declines in the white population and immigration restrictions (Frey, 2021). The nation is also increasingly racially and ethnically diverse, with people of color representing 80% of population growth since 2000 (Frey, 2018). At the same time, the nation has experienced unprecedented racial conflict and protest, particularly since the murders of George Floyd and Breonna Taylor. While many have protested in support of and in demanding racial justice and equity, others have waged war against it. Most recently, several states have implemented "gag order legislation" following Donald Trump's since rescinded executive order against critical race theory and diversity trainings. In the first

TABLE I.1
Community College Enrollment by Race, Fall 2019

White	Latinx	Black	Asian/Pacific Islander	Native American	Two or More Races
44%	27%	13%	6%	1%	4%

Note: From AACC (2021).

6 months following the end of Trump's one-term presidency, 23 states introduced legislation to limit teaching of the United States' racial history. As of this writing this is up to 36. At least 14 states have passed such legislation (African American Policy Forum, 2021), further threatening our democracy by limiting the ability of educational institutions to discuss the realities of racial inequities.

The COVID-19 pandemic brought additional racial inequities to light while also accelerating the pace of changes in the nature and expectations of work. Technological advances and a digital platform economy have transformed some work environments to be more flexible and online. Uncertainty about the impact of this new economy remains, as work schedules may become fragmented and part-time contract work may increase (Kenney & Zysman, 2016), leading to hesitancy and risk in the labor market even before the COVID-19 outbreak (Cutolo & Kenney, 2020). Notably, as work has become increasingly remote and online, many community college students have not had consistent access to stable Wi-Fi or adequate technology.

While the long-term impacts of this persistent health crisis have yet to be seen, it is clear that it has put additional pressure on the economy and workforce. Millions of people lost their jobs or experienced income reductions, with Black and Brown people, women, and those who are less formally educated at the greatest risk of job loss (Shah, 2021). Unlike in previous years, when an economic downturn meant a spike in college enrollment for new job training (particularly in the community college sector), those un- or underemployed during the pandemic have not sought to enroll in college for additional or new training. While enrollment in community colleges has been declining over the past decade, enrollment dropped in spring 2021 by more than 11% compared to 1 year earlier (National Student Clearinghouse Research Center, 2021). The economic strain on community colleges has therefore grown in recent years.

Leadership and Fiscal Challenges

With so much uncertainty in the workforce and in society writ large, community colleges need federal and state support more than ever. Although enrollment has declined in recent years, policymakers continue to expect community colleges to fix the economy by developing a skilled labor force. Largely, community colleges have met or exceeded workforce demands. Nationally, community colleges enroll and train nearly 80% of all first responders (including police officers, EMTs, and firefighters), and they graduate more than half of new nurses and health-care workers (National Commission on Community Colleges, 2008). It is estimated that 62% of all job openings between 2019 and 2029 will require at least some college, with nursing and health-care positions among the fastest growing occupations (Torpey, 2020). Given the size and variation of the populations that community colleges serve and the economic needs of their communities, they, more than any other sector of higher education, must be responsive to policymaker demands and community needs. And more than most other institutions, they will need to do so quickly and with fewer resources.

Community colleges serve an academically, racially, and economically diverse student body and maintain an equally diverse mission. Yet, they consistently have been underfunded when compared to four-year colleges that serve a less diverse student population (The Institute for College Access and Success, 2019). Demands for accountability and efficiency have grown as policymakers seek to increase degree completion and vocation credentialing. There is, however, no evidence to support claims that community colleges have become less efficient (Belfield & Jenkins, 2014). Still the rhetoric has negative consequences for community colleges, as Belfield and Jenkins (2014) argue:

> The notion that higher education institutions are squandering resources, which is now commonplace both in public discourse and in the policy arena, influences decisions about funding allocations across the sector (by making it easier to reduce public subsidies under the rationale that colleges are inefficient). It also influences students' views about whether to attend college, particularly among students who are debt-averse or who have no family experience of college-going. (p. 1)

Between 2006 and 2016, state funding per student slightly increased at community colleges while remaining level or declining at public four-year institutions. Still, community colleges lag behind doctoral institutions in state funding by nearly $2,900 per student. In 2016, community colleges could "spend 61 cents for every dollar institutions offering master's degrees could spend—two pennies more than a decade earlier" (Murakami, 2020, para. 14).

State funding is critically important as it is community colleges' primary source (33.7%) of revenue (AACC, 2021). Colleges and universities generally offset reductions in state appropriations by increasing tuition. Indeed, per-student tuition revenue increased across all sectors of higher education in the decade between 2006 and 2016 (TICAS, 2019). Revenue at doctoral- and master's-granting institutions remained level. By increasing tuition, four-year institutions increased their revenue by 19% in the same decade. Total revenue at community colleges, however, declined by 5% due to their inability to increase tuition. During academic year 2020–2021, public community colleges, on average, charged less than $4,000 for tuition, while public four-year colleges charged more than $10,500 for in-state tuition (AACC, 2021).

In addition, community colleges, unlike research-intensive institutions, have few alternative sources of revenue (i.e., endowments, research facilities, etc.). Few community colleges offer meal plans and/or on-campus housing. In fact, total revenue for community colleges in 2016 was just 37% of doctoral universities (TICAS, 2019). These inequities in funding combined with declining enrollments and relatively fixed tuition negatively impact community college leaders' ability to fulfill their institutional missions, state goals, and community expectations.

This is the challenge of those who lead and work in community colleges: to increase educational opportunities and successes in the face of decreased funding and increased accountability. To meet the expectations of policymakers and the general public, and to fulfill their institutional missions, community colleges require stable and committed leadership, which in itself is a challenge. Certainly, leading any institution of higher education is arduous. In 2016, the average tenure of a college president was 6.5 years (as cited in Artis & Bartel, 2021). Twenty years ago, Schults (2001) found that 45% of community college presidents planned to retire within 6 years. In 2021, "community colleges are still scrambling to find leaders poised and ready to take on the dynamic and challenging environment of community college leadership" (Artis & Bartel, 2021, p. 1). Fortunately, those who choose to lead have demonstrated some optimism about the future of community colleges, as 92% believe the Biden–Harris administration's policies will positively impact their institutions (Jaschik & Lederman, 2021). Eighty-one percent of community college presidents believe it is more important for their institutions to address racial inequities now than in previous years, suggesting more leaders recognize the need to support a diverse democracy.

The lack of state investment, however, places the equity and opportunity goals further at risk. Community colleges, primarily open-access institutions, are tasked with being the democratizing arm of the higher education system (Dowd, 2003) while states have pushed for accountability and efficiency. To meet the needs of the students who enroll in the community college and to support two-year institutions in serving their communities, state and local governments must provide more balance between equity and efficiency goals (Dowd & Shieh, 2013). Indeed, as Bob has argued and as Josh Wyner echoed,

> As [community colleges] go, so goes the country. . . . And so go communities. . . . Without them, we're really going to be hard-pressed to make good on the promise of equal opportunity for a good life and a good career. (Anderson & Douglas-Gabriel, 2021, para. 17)

Overview of the Book

In this book, we argue that higher education must be a key stakeholder in building and sustaining the communities of America and believe community colleges are committed to each of those ends. In so doing, we demonstrate ways community colleges seek to make good on higher education's promise to build our nation's democracy, one student at a time. We also show that the collective work of the faculty and staff of the community college movement is not only to prepare students to transfer and/or to enter the workforce. It is also their collective purpose to prepare students for active and engaged citizenship, understanding that the outcome of a strong education is a stronger democracy. Indeed, students with some college or associate degrees are more likely than those with only a high school diploma to volunteer in community organizations and to support a political candidate (Newell, 2014).

Through storytelling, personal narrative, scholarship review, and focused questions, we hope to provide higher education leaders, policymakers, and scholars (particularly, but not limited to those in community colleges) additional insight into the important role community colleges play as key stakeholders in the development of educated and informed society and a sustainable community. Each chapter is built on stories from the field based on Bob's career teaching and leading in the community college movement. Each story is designed to illuminate a specific and significant aspect of the community college experience and has implications for current and aspiring leaders in higher education. All chapters conclude with Tara's clarifying comments, critical reflections, and questions for the reader to consider their role in creating change. The questions posed at the end of each chapter reflection may be particularly useful for graduate students of higher education or trainings for higher education leadership. It is our working assumption that storytelling balanced with extant scholarship and critical reflection provides the reader with powerful opportunities for learning and for taking action.

Grounded in the work of John Dewey, chapter 1 sets the philosophical framework for the book; it is the inexorable link between education, community, and democracy. Bob's personal narrative and storytelling about his experiences at Greenfield Community College (GCC) illuminate many aspects of those connections. Chapter 2 provides the historical and cultural context of the community college movement. The significance of President Truman's 1947 Commission on Higher Education as well as the development of Joliet Junior College are highlighted. In this chapter we also look at the concept of border crossing as both a metaphor and reality for many community college students.

Chapter 3 tells the stories of community and why building it is essential to serving it. Bob provides examples of why and how community building, on and off campus, serves students, faculty, staff, as well as the external community. We propose that our democracy is weaker without strong communities, adding that education must be a key stakeholder toward that end. Tara's reflections require us to consider what racial profiling looks like in community colleges and how, if not acknowledged, it will damage any efforts to create an inclusive campus climate.

Chapter 4 is a discussion about leadership. In this chapter, we suggest that current models of leadership often taught in graduate programs are not as effective as is needed for today's challenges or tomorrow's uncertainty. Topics include mission, culture, environment formation, facilities planning, resource development, accreditation, betterment, crisis management, and governance. The reflection at the end of the chapter also speaks to the importance of college leaders and community members having ownership of their institutions and creating a welcoming space for all students, particularly those underserved.

In Part Two, we share stories from the field, based on Bob's personal and sometimes virtual visits to five different community colleges across the country. Each college represents different geographic regions and institutional sizes (from more than 2,000 students to more than 14,000). Most importantly, each campus also highlights different foci that establish these unique institutions as anchors of democracy in their various communities, whether rural or urban. It is important to note that several of the colleges we highlight now offer baccalaureate degrees and may or may not have *community* in their institutional names. Still, community is always present, and the members of their communities, on and off campus, recognize the significance of their college's mission to serve their respective regions.

Chapter 5 tells the story of the long-standing, small, and rural Connors State College (CSC) in Oklahoma. Bob's visit along with Tara's reflections about rural and urban colleges speak to the challenges and impact of anchor colleges in the community. Chapter 6 tells the story of Hostos Community College in the South Bronx, New York, the poorest congressional district in the United States. As the story of Hostos unfolds, it provides a snapshot and example of all that we discuss in the book, a true anchor of the community working toward a true democracy.

Chapter 7 tells the story of Grand Rapids Community College (GRCC) in Michigan. Both Massachusetts and Michigan declared states of emergency due to COVID-19 just as we were scheduled to depart for a visit to Grand Rapids. It was the first of three virtual visits. Although not as holistic an experience as an in-person visit, it became most evident in every Zoom call that GRCC is a most "responsive and relevant" large urban college.

Chapter 8 tells the story of Diné College in Tsaile, Arizona, the first Tribal College in the United States. There was a warmth of spirit there that Bob found familiar yet all too distant. It is the way of *K'e* that is core to the Navajo Nation culture and core to the Diné College experience. Diné is a college created by Navajo people to serve the people and communities of the Navajo Nation. While Diné College tells a story of resistance, we also considered the painful history of the United States government-sanctioned schools that sought to erase Native Americans and their culture. This chapter demonstrates how Diné seeks to preserve their culture.

Chapter 9 describes Bob's virtual visit to Berkeley City College in Berkeley, California. Berkeley City College was built in the heart of the city. On a map it looks like it is situated in the economic center of Berkeley, directly between Berkeley High School and the University of California at Berkeley. It seems purposeful, an almost perfect metaphor. Education and jobs, education and civic engagement, education and economic mobility, education and liberty—education and democracy, one building and yet so many powerful outcomes. Like most community colleges, Berkeley City College represents a story worth telling but is often overlooked. Chapter 10 provides a few concluding thoughts and recommendations.

John Dewey gave a speech in 1902 about the importance of schools being the social center of a community. It was a significant and compelling talk that could have been presented today, its relevance as current to the challenges of 2022 as 1902. Dewey tells the crowd of educators, "The pressing thing, the significant thing, is really to make the school a social center; that is a matter of practice, not of theory . . . to bring it completely into the current of social life" (p. 73). He concludes by stating, "We may say that the conception of the school as a social center is born of our entire democratic movement" (p. 73). Core to our ability to realize democracy is the relationship between education and community. No segment of higher education has embraced that mission more so than the community college. We wrote this book to further illustrate and tell the story of these public two-year institutions as anchors of democracy, the community's colleges.

PART ONE

FOUNDATIONS

EDUCATION, COMMUNITY, AND DEMOCRACY

We grow accustomed to the dark, when light is put away.

—Emily Dickinson

When the magistrate of Family and Probate Court called there was a somber tone to his voice. He had called many times over the course of 18 years about many different projects, but his voice was different this time: "Bob, we need to do something about the opioid problem in our community." He added, "The Sheriff, District Attorney, and I would like to invite a few people together to discuss the problem and think about solutions. We want to meet in your office." "Of course," I replied, "We are in."

After a few meetings with 10, then 50, then 100 local leaders, the Franklin County Opioid Task Force (OTF) was formed, and it had a home base. GCC became engaged in the community's opioid problem by building relationships and creating a pathway from the recovery community to the college, working with leaders in the court system, creating courses for inmates at the county jail, developing post-incarceration workforce programs, establishing a recovery community on campus, and creating an Addiction Studies Certificate program to strengthen the workforce pipeline. GCC took a seat at the leadership table.

The community came together to respond to a community problem and GCC was one of the many key stakeholders. Those three leaders of the OTF called on the college because they understood that GCC was the community's college, one that John Dewey (1902) would suggest was "completely into the current of social life . . . as a matter of practice, not of theory" (p. 73).

That short narrative serves to frame the purpose of this book, to tell the story and elevate the role of community colleges, who in addition to maintaining an open-door admissions policy are significant partners and key stakeholders in the development and sustainability of community. In so doing, community colleges are fulfilling our nation's historic mission of educating for democracy.

A Story From the Field

As you drive onto the GCC campus you can't help but notice the foothills of the Berkshire mountains that provide a warm embrace for the college's buildings and grounds. The peak colors of fall frame the campus, not unlike that of a Monet or Van Gogh. Just to the north is farmland, feed for the occasional cow. Off to the right of the college's half-mile driveway are two large fields, grass growing on some of the richest soil in America. Those are the same fields where 8,000 people gather every summer for the Green River Music and Balloon Festival and hundreds every fall for the community's youth soccer league.

I would always take a moment to enjoy the view from the commencement tent that sits on the upper field on the first Saturday of every June. The cows would wander on the north side of the fence a few feet from the solar energy panels as students walked across the platform about to graduate; it was classic GCC. At the center of the campus is the duck pond, often a reminder that a pebble can have more of an impact in a small pond than a boulder tossed into the ocean. The metaphor fit our experience.

Many of the farms that dot the landscape of the Western Massachusetts community are family owned. Like all the institutions and businesses in Franklin County, the farms are small, especially in comparison to those of the Midwest. The economies of scale have an enormous impact on everything and in every way in the community. It is both an opportunity and a challenge in education as much as it is in business. While there is great opportunity to provide personalized quality service, the challenge to make the numbers work is daunting.

I loved that we were able to form-fit education to each student at the college as best we could, but the per-student costs in rural America are creating a death spiral for some schools and colleges. State funding has not kept pace with the costs of doing business in public education at the same time we are experiencing steep population decline. Those same fiscal dynamics exist in the private sector. The economies of scale eventually force schools to offer less, which in turn drives parents and students to move to another town or choice into schools that do offer those lost activities, classes, sports, music, or the like. As those families move away from those schools, the educational opportunities they were looking for increasingly move with them. The downward spiral continues. Although private prep schools like Deerfield Academy, Northfield Mount Hermon, and the Stoneleigh Burnham School for Girls, with all their wealth of opportunity, have resided in the community for hundreds of years, they might as well have been in another universe.

The annual Franklin County Fair Parade was a perfect reflection of Franklin County. It was pure Americana, not unlike the music genre of the same name. I even had the honor of being the parade marshal one year. People from all neighborhoods, towns, and walks of life would line the streets of downtown Greenfield. It was pure small-town rural America, and it was beautiful.

GCC students, alumni, faculty, and staff would march in the parade to the shouts of those good people showing their appreciation of the college. Reporter Richie Davis of the *Greenfield Recorder* wrote the quintessential articles about the community, especially those local family-run farms. As Davis (2019) tells it, "Franklin County is all-natural, down-home New England, where real-life stories abound" (para. 4).

The documentary *Root Hog or Die*, by local moviemaker Rawn Fuller, also tells the story of those farms, the families, and their lifestyle in black and white. Watching the town's fight against Walmart in the movie *Talking to the Wall* is yet another part of the landscape of the community. A colleague once told me that he would hear roosters, cows, and NPR flow from the houses along his route as he peddled his way to the campus during Ride a Bike to GCC Week. Each are meditations of Franklin County, the smallest, most rural, and poorest county in the Commonwealth of Massachusetts.

Many who live in Franklin County came to Western Massachusetts to attend one of the "Five Colleges" (Amherst, Hampshire, Mount Holyoke, Smith Colleges, and University of Massachusetts [UMass] Amherst) and never left. They chose a lifestyle more than a lucrative livelihood. But finding a physician who would forgo that big city salary for service in small, poor, rural communities is not as easy. Others were born and raised in the community, maybe three or four generations of one family living just a brief ride from town to town along the Deerfield River. Many live there by choice, while others are stuck in the muck and mire of working poverty.

GCC faculty and staff might have come to the college looking for a job, but all who stayed found something larger: purpose, meaning, and pumpernickel passion. They also found community.

Students drive to GCC down the Mohawk Trail from the beautiful hill towns of "West County," many eager to become a nurse, police officer, EMT, or firefighter. Others come from the low-lying towns along the river wanting to teach in the community in which they grew up and where they are eager to raise their own family. Some come to learn about manufacturing, technology, and business while others are excited to understand a better way to move food from farm to table. Still others come to see if their talent for art-making is as strong as their passion for it.

Some students come enthusiastic to become leaders in the recreational waters and on the mountains of the great outdoors, and still others come to understand more about alternative energy systems, sustainability, and the environment. Learning about the environment at GCC is akin to studying oceanography on an island. Some students are eager to join the workforce as soon as possible while others look to GCC as a step on a longer journey toward transferring and earning a baccalaureate degree.

Many came to GCC in pursuit of a dream that they did not understand, that was not yet clearly defined. All come to GCC, a bright light in the wilderness of rural poverty, in the pursuit of a better life.

Most students at GCC are the first generation in their family to attend college, and over 45% are Pell eligible. Sixty-two percent identify as female, 38% male, 22% students of color; 69% attend part-time and 31% full-time. Their average age is 27, and the median is 23. GCC awarded 358 degrees and certificates in 2019. The GCC faculty-to-student ratio is 12:1, and 36% of the students receive $6.1 million in financial aid, including $2.2 million in federal student loans. Those are some of the numbers; here are eight examples of the 8 million stories of community college students across America.

Jake dropped out of high school. He was a drug addict. After months of aimless missteps, Jake began his journey to recovery, leading him back to education and the GED. Because of GCC's good relationship with the Literacy Project, the community's long-standing adult education program, he took one class at the college, then another, then earned the AA degree. Jake eventually received a full scholarship to attend Amherst College and went on to the University of Oregon where he earned his MFA. I am not yet sure if Jake's talents will lead him to write that great American novel, to teach, or both.

Hawa came to GCC from Sierra Leone in part because of the guidance and support of a GCC Foundation board member. I will never forget the intensity of Hawa's reaction when I told her she was accepted at Smith College with a full scholarship. She broke down in my office that day because she knew that her work at GCC and Smith would help her create the school for girls in her village she had always dreamed about. Hawa is working to force cultural change regarding the murder and rape of the girls and women of Sierra Leone.

Jody really didn't know what she wanted to do with her life as a high school senior. After a few conversations with her counselor, she decided to enroll at GCC. Because tuition was affordable, she had the opportunity to explore and take classes in different fields. Jody found her calling in law enforcement at GCC and became the first woman police chief for the city of Northampton.

Simon's talent as a musician is far beyond his years. He seems to channel an older soul when playing music. You will soon want to purchase a ticket to one of his concerts. Although he came to GCC challenged by his lack of sight, Simon left with a full scholarship to UMass Amherst to further develop his amazing talents. His 4.0 GPA at graduation was a clear indication to all of us at GCC that Simon's genius was not limited to the piano.

Rosemarie and Heather were single moms with a great deal of courage, intelligence, and bills to pay, but no money. Then the doors to the college were opened to both. Not only did they find the support they needed at GCC, but they also received Francis Perkins and Ada Comstock scholarships to Mount Holyoke and Smith Colleges, respectively. Today, both are leaders in education, human services, and social justice in the Franklin County community.

Jean graduated from the very first nursing class at GCC. She later became the long-standing director of the program. Jean is one of the thousands of women and men who have graduated from the GCC Nursing program, who all assumed positions at the hospitals and health care facilities of Western Massachusetts and became vested in the health and well-being of the community.

Robbie was a "loser," and he loves saying that about himself. He was smart enough but lost his way. Soon after a work accident in the food industry in Boston, Robbie came home to Greenfield. His mother made him go to GCC: "Just go down to that new college and see what they have to offer." Robbie found himself and graduated from GCC and then from the University of Denver. As a very successful local business leader and philanthropist, Robbie became chair of the GCC Board of Trustees and was named the 2020 Recorder Citizen of the Year. Robbie is often quoted, "If it wasn't for GCC, I would still be lost and still be a loser."

It is hard to believe that GCC's beautiful campus is in the center of the poorest county in the commonwealth. But the truth is that you won't find many community colleges in affluent communities. That is why the grounds crew took better care of the college than their own homes. That is why students, faculty, staff, and community feel such pride in GCC.

I remember giving a visitor a tour around the college and the community. She had just taken a position at one of the Five Colleges. I could tell something was weighing heavily on her. "Are you okay?" I asked. "Well, no, not really," she replied. "I haven't seen this kind of poverty since I left the

Appalachians." Maybe it is because of its hard-working farming roots, or blue-collar manufacturing base, but Franklin County is also one of the most collaborative communities I know of when responding to its challenges, and GCC is a key stakeholder and essential partner in that work.

Local business leader, community leader, and GCC Trustee Tim Farrell once said at a board meeting in 2018:

> I have had the honor of serving as Chair of the Board of Trustees at GCC, Chair of the School Committee for the Greenfield Public Schools, President of the Greenfield Town Council and serve on various other public and private boards. I grew up in Greenfield, live here now, own a local insurance agency, and raise my two kids in this town. The one constant, in all those settings and in all that work, has been the importance of GCC to this community.

All who have driven down College Drive since GCC opened its doors in 1962 have felt its transformative power; so has the community it serves.

Linking education to the needs of students as well as community is core to the community college movement. From its inception, community colleges have been inexorably tied to the building and development of community. That relationship, between college and community, elevates the economic and social well-being of students, families, and community. In so doing, the foundations of our democracy are stronger and more sustainable.

Education, Community, and Democracy

Without strong communities, a nation is built on a house of cards. Education must be a key stakeholder in building and sustaining the communities of America. Access to a college degree provides the pathway to a better life for students and their families. Communities across this nation are just as dependent on those colleges to provide the engaged and educated citizenry, as well as the workforce, that is needed for a better future.

Too many Americans are "living on the outskirts of hope" (NPR News, 2014, para. 10), working and poor, place-bound, homebound, and unable to leave their community because of family, work, and economic realities. They are economically, socially, academically, and systemically diverted away from higher education and the dreams of a better life. Families, communities, the economy, and our democracy are weaker as a result. The interdependence of a college education with good jobs at family-sustaining wages, social and economic mobility, an educated workforce citizenry, sustainable communities, and a strong democracy is increasingly clear.

John Dewey gave a speech in October 1902 at a National Education Association conference in Chicago to public school teachers about the importance of schools being the social center of a community. It was a significant and compelling talk that could have been presented today, its relevance as current to the challenges of 2022 as it was in 1902. Dewey tells the crowd of educators, "The pressing thing, the significant thing, is really to make the school a social center; that is, a matter of practice, not of theory . . . to bring it completely into the current of social life" (para. 1).

Later in that speech Dewey emphasizes that

> No educational system can be regarded as complete until it adopts into itself the various ways in which social and intellectual intercourse may be promoted, and employs them systematically, not only to counteract dangers which these same agencies are bringing with them, but so as to make them positive causes in raising the whole level of life. (para. 23)

John Dewey concludes his speech by stating, "We may say that the conception of the school as a social center is born of our entire democratic movement" (para. 24). Core to a sustaining democracy is education firmly rooted at the core of community.

In their article "The Enduring Appeal of Community Schools," Benson et al. (2009) wrote, "Community schools are an old American idea . . . based on two premises: that the purpose of schooling is to educate youth for democratic citizenship, and that schools and communities are inextricably inter-twined and interdependent" (p. 22). Dewey (1902) added,

> Everywhere we see signs of the growing recognition that the community owes to each one of its members the fullest opportunity for development . . . education has always been a community endeavor. (p. 39)

In *Dewey's Dream*, Benson et al. (2007) make the point that in addition to Dewey's seminal work on pragmatism, democracy, and education, one of his most significant and lasting contributions is that of the community school: "Democracy must begin at home," wrote Dewey in 1916, adding "its home is the neighborly community" (p. 54). Democracy's home is in community, and education is the front door.

And then in *Knowledge for Social Change: Bacon, Dewey, and the Revolutionary Transformation of Research Universities in the Twenty-First Century*, Benson et al. (2017) further emphasize the need for community-based education: "The higher education democratic civic and community engagement movement emphasizes that collaboration inside and outside the academy is necessary for producing knowledge that solves real-world problems and results in positive changes in the human condition" (p. 69).

I learned a great deal and enjoyed reading each of those works by Benson and his colleagues. Clearly, they get it, and they teach it (education + community = democracy). I found it remarkable, however, truly remarkable, that although the focus of those publications and their work at the University of Pennsylvania is to encourage a stronger relationship between higher education and community, the authors never mention community colleges.

How could that be? No institutional segment of higher education has been more engaged in the development and sustainability of community— its hopes, dreams, challenges, and solutions—than the community colleges of the United States of America.

Higher Education's Responsibility

I remember attending a gallery talk at GCC presented by a photographer from southern Vermont who worked with digital cameras. It is a story that I have shared on many occasions and one that appeared in *The Recorder*. Toward the end of his presentation a student asked the artist, "Could you have taken the same photographs and had the same show with film?" The response was, "Yes—but it would have been different." He went on to point out that some of Hollywood's best directors such as Steven Spielberg and Quentin Tarantino use film only.

That gallery talk caused me to think about my music collection over the years and about how the quality of the sound itself had changed as well. Just as the photographer suggested that images captured digitally would be different than those on film, I thought music recorded and listened to digitally must be different from analog/high-fidelity recordings, the latter producing a fuller, more nuanced, and complex sound. That must be the reason why Spielberg and Tarantino use just film. It is about the nuances and the depth as opposed to the binary experience.

Merriam-Webster (n.d.) defines *binary* as "consisting of, indicating, or involving two." It is the foundation of all computing and digital technology. Our phones, desktops, TVs, radios, watches, and many kitchen appliances are all run by binary systems that simplify the coding to either on or off. That's it, on and off.

That binary process has seemingly seeped into our economic, political, social, intellectual, and educational institutions. It is as if our whole way of thinking and acting have become binary. Things have become either right or wrong, good or bad, rich or poor, have or have not, black or white—on or off. We live in binary times.

A binary economy has created binary communities, binary politics, binary thinking, and increasingly binary education systems. All too often we are pressed into binary decisions that produce binary outcomes, with no apparent tolerance for nuance or complexity. Those binary practices undermine collaboration, community, and ultimately our democracy.

At a time of expanding binary systems and escalating binary thinking, of increasing isolation and decreasing hope; at a time when our nation does not seem to act on its stated egalitarian values, our democracy and the education that supports it are under attack, weakening the foundations on which we stand, in the pursuit of liberty and justice for all. Our nation's schools and colleges must strive for something better (Pura, 2016; Solomon, 2018).

Massachusetts Secretary of Education Horace Mann, in his Report No. 12 of the Massachusetts School Board in 1848 (Cremin, 1957), wrote,

> According to the European theory, men are divided into classes, some to toil and earn, others to seize and enjoy. According to Massachusetts' theory, all are to have an equal chance for earning, and equal security in the enjoyment of what they earn . . . [which] is the highest duty of a state. (pp. 79–80)

Later in that report he writes, "Education, then, beyond all other devices of human origin, is a great equalizer of the conditions of men—the balance wheel of the social machinery." (pp. 79–80)

Those are the same ideals, values, and principles that Governor Foster Furcolo brought to the creation of the community colleges of the Commonwealth of Massachusetts. "I always thought it would be the salvation of most of our families," said Governor Foster Furcolo, the author of the community college system in Massachusetts. Having grown up in affluent Longmeadow, Massachusetts, Furcolo added that he remembers "being bothered by the fact that some of [his] fellow students could not afford to go on to higher education, and that seemed very unfair" (paras. 5, 7). Those are also the same core values that community colleges around the nation were committed to when they opened their doors in service to students and community (Carlock, 1986).

Education is not only the foundation of our democracy; it is also the bedrock of our liberty. In *Narrative of the Life of Frederick Douglass* (1845), Douglas, enslaved as a child, wrote of his experience one night while listening to his so-called master. His enslaver said, "If you teach the slave how to read, there would be no keeping him. It would forever unfit him to be a slave.

He would at once become unmanageable and of no value to his master"
(p. 33). Education was a threat to the slave industry because it encouraged
people to use their minds and think for themselves and because those who
were enslaved would learn about uprisings and would understand how to
fight for freedom.

Democracy can never be realized in a separate and inequitable society;
it is the outcome of a nation's collective commitment to provide an excellent
education for all. Education at its best does not occur behind an ivy wall
separate from the realities of everyday life; rather, education must be an integrated fiber in the tapestry of community. Our community colleges hold out
that lantern and provide hope for students, their families, and the communities of our nation. The collective work of the faculty and staff of our nations'
community colleges then is not only to prepare students to transfer and for
the workforce. It is also their collective purpose to prepare students for active
and engaged citizenship, understanding that the outcome of a strong education is a stronger democracy.

The founding mothers and fathers of our nation understood that education was a public good and were inspired to tax themselves to support and
invest in it. Built on its core values of equity and excellence, no segment of
higher education has embraced the mantle of "Democracy's College" more
so than the community colleges of America.

In her article "From Access to Outcome Equity: Revitalizing the
Democratic Mission of the Community College," Alicia Dowd (2003) wrote,
"The two-year public sector is the primary point of entry into higher
education for low-income students, African Americans, Latinos, immigrants,
and working adults" (p. 1).

By expanding higher education's enrollment capacity, community colleges are understood by many as playing an important democratizing role
in the American postsecondary system. With open admissions policies and
diverse student bodies, community colleges "in an idealized sense, represent
higher education's commitment to democracy" (Rhoads & Valadez, 1996,
p. 7).

I wanted to see what the oldest college in the nation thought about
democracy, liberty, and education. Harvard University Faculty of Arts and
Sciences (2007) states:

> A Harvard education is a liberal education. . . . It is preparation for the
> rest of life. The subjects that undergraduates study and, as importantly,
> the skills and habits of mind they acquire in the process, shape the lives
> they will lead after they leave the academy. . . . All of them (our students)
> will be citizens, whether of the United States or another country, and as
> such will be helping to make decisions that may affect the lives of oth-
> ers. All of them will engage with forces of change—cultural, religious,

political, demographic, technological, planetary. All of them will have to assess empirical claims, interpret cultural expressions, and confront ethical dilemmas in their personal and professional lives. A liberal education gives students the tools to face these challenges in an informed and thoughtful way. (p. 1).

The root of the words *liberal* and *liberty* comes from the Latin "liber," which means "free." Community college students deserve no less access to liberty and freedom and no less a preparation for the demands of an engaged life as the students at Harvard University. In fact, without access to those opportunities, our nation's democracy is in peril.

The need cannot be overstated. The strength and sustainability of our nation is dependent on the strength and sustainability of the communities of the United States. The strength and sustainability of community is dependent on higher education and an engaged and educated citizenry. Community colleges have, from their first entry to the higher education landscape, embraced that mission and accepted that responsibility.

Reflections

In this first chapter, Bob lays the foundation for the remainder of the book. By highlighting the significance of the community college as a "social center," Bob also pushes us to understand what we mean by democracy. He states that democracy "is the outcome of a nation's collective commitment to provide an excellent education for all." Community colleges support a more equitable democracy by preparing students for further education via transfer and preparing students for future employment or developing new skills while also preparing students to be active and contributing citizens. At the same time, higher education institutions, and specifically community colleges, must be more than even that. In an interview with the American Council on Education's (2019) *Higher Education Today*, University of California, Los Angeles Professor Sylvia Hurtado argued higher education must reflect "the society we aspire to become." She went on to say that instead of perpetuating the racial and economic disparities that exist in society, higher education must "create greater equity and a more diverse democracy" (para. 1).

Community colleges are instrumental in these efforts as their diverse mission requires them to serve adult students looking for vocational skills and training, as well as recent high school graduates, many of whom had inequitable educational experiences due to attending segregated and/or under-resourced schools. Community colleges, then, have an opportunity and perhaps an obligation to do what Hurtado implores higher education to do: "push the restart button and rethink the way the world works" (American Council on Education, 2019, para. 2). They, perhaps more than any other sector in higher education, are responsible for upholding or creating a diverse democracy.

Community colleges enroll a highly diverse student body representing more than 12 million students in over 1,100 institutions (including those that offer a bachelor's degree; CCRC, 2020). Nearly half (49%) of all students who complete a four-year degree once attended a community college. Clearly, community colleges play a fundamental role in efforts to increase degree completion. At the same time, community colleges are some of the most underfunded and under-resourced colleges in the nation (The Institute for College Access and Success [TICAS], 2019). Despite their importance to college access, degree completion, and democracy itself, state funding for these institutions has not kept pace with the investment that millions of students make in this sector of higher education.

Community colleges are thus challenged to democratize the higher education system (Dowd, 2003) by facilitating educational opportunities and building student successes, while also facing decreased state support. In addition to improving workforce development and transfer, and degree completion rates, higher education system leaders and state and local policymakers increasingly call on community colleges to reform developmental education and improve educational quality overall. Limited fiscal resources, however, restrict access and higher education's ability to meet democratic goals (Dowd & Shieh, 2013).

If state and local governments are serious about student success and two-year institutions being a resource to their communities, policymakers must do a better job of balancing equity and efficiency goals (Dowd & Shieh, 2013). Despite enrolling half of all undergraduates of color and half of all undergraduates who ever complete a baccalaureate degree, states fiscally support community colleges at two thirds the rate of four-year public universities. Even when states can afford to better fund community colleges, they do not (Koh et al., 2019). While access remains important to community colleges, states have virtually required community colleges to "do more with less." Public funds have decreased, which threatens access and limits community colleges in achieving outcomes that support students in meeting their aspirational goals, improving transfer, and degree completion. It also limits community colleges' ability to offer cultural and educational resources to the larger community. Indeed, reduced state appropriations and reductions in other fiscal supports "are the real killers" of access for students of color (Bell, 2004, p. 159). State lawmakers and institutional leaders would do well to recall this statement from earlier in this chapter:

> Without strong communities, a nation is built on a house of cards. Education must be a key stakeholder in building and sustaining the communities of America. Access to a college degree provides the pathway to a better life for students and their families. Communities across this nation are just as dependent on those colleges to provide the engaged and educated citizenry, as well as the workforce, that is needed for a better future. (p. 18)

Some years ago, a community college president shared with me that his greatest fear was that there would be two tiers of higher education: one that privileges wealthy, white, and native-born citizens while disadvantaging those who are poor, immigrants, and/or people of color. The haves will have access to bachelor's and advanced degrees while the have-nots will have nothing more than a "smattering of education." Indeed, the stratification of higher education remains a concern for those interested in access, equity, and democracy.

Nearly four million students enroll in community colleges in urban areas or large cities. Because urban community colleges serve even more diverse student populations, they are also vital to serving as "democracy's colleges." As Myran and Parsons (2013) indicate, the "failure of opportunity" is most evident in urban centers, as they offer great opportunity and great loss. Cities are cultural centers and economic engines at the same time they are centers of "racial and economic isolation, poverty" (p. 8), and deferred dreams. Because of the racial, ethnic, and economic diversity of cities and urban areas, urban community colleges have a particular responsibility to promote racial and economic equity. They must not only develop the community's workforce, but they must be a part of social change in that community.

Urban community colleges are therefore key to a "multiracial democracy" by promoting social and racial justice and gender and civic equity and by developing the voices of those most underserved. Although not exclusively, the recent racial uprisings in the wake of George Floyd's murder have taken place primarily in cities across the United States. Community colleges have responded with town halls examining the origins of the racial pandemic (Grand Rapids Community College), scholarships to support efforts toward racial equity (Copper Mountain College), and rethinking the ways they train police officers (California, Minnesota, and Virginia community college systems). These initiatives, however, run the risk of being limited in scope, scale, and duration. To address the needs of urban centers and rural communities, community colleges will need to be ready and willing to take on the task of promoting racial and social justice.

Institutional leaders would do well to turn their attention to chronic budget reductions and other issues that impact resources at community colleges, particularly when facing an economic downturn. Most community college students enter with the desire to complete a baccalaureate degree (Conway, 2010). Administration, faculty, and staff must be prepared to assist them in reaching those goals. Institutional leaders, therefore, must be prepared to advocate for community colleges and support those who work, teach, and learn in them if we are serious about creating an equitable democracy.

Discussion Questions

1. Chapter 1 told the story of one community college, and it holds implications for many other community colleges across the United States (whether rural, urban, or suburban). Often these are untold stories. Reflect on the stories you heard about community colleges. Are there common themes to the stories? What stories need to be told more often and more loudly? Which ones need to change?

2. In this chapter, Bob argued, "The strength and sustainability of the nation is dependent on the strength and sustainability of community. The strength and sustainability of community is dependent on higher education and an engaged and educated citizenry." What role does the community college play in strengthening and sustaining community? What responsibility does the community college have in creating an equitable democracy?

3. What did Foster Furcolo mean when he said, "I always thought [community colleges] would be the salvation of most of our families?"

4. What is the impact of underfunding community colleges on communities? On students of color? What examples can you point to that demonstrate this impact?

5. In what ways might a state better balance equity and efficiency? How should institutional leadership balance equity and efficiency?

2

THE COMMUNITY
COLLEGE MOVEMENT

I lift my lamp beside the golden door.

—Emma Lazarus

My dad was an immigrant. He came to this country through the doors of Ellis Island. I remember walking up the very same steps he did as a child soon after the Ellis Island Museum had opened. The weight of the moment unexpectedly buckled my knees. As you walk up the main staircase, you enter the great room with floor to ceiling windows. Off to the right was the most majestic symbol of liberty and democracy in the world. Off to the left, the skyline of a nation and all of its opportunities. The distance between the two, between access and opportunity, is a gap too large for anyone to swim alone. A vessel is needed, and such is the role and responsibility of education. To paraphrase poet Emily Dickenson, there truly is no frigate like education. For about half of all who have entered higher education, it is the community college movement that has held out the lamp for all who are yearning to breathe free. It is in the journey from access to acquiring the skills and knowledge necessary to succeed, that lives are changed for the better, families and community then grow stronger, and as a result, so too our democracy.

Dad never did graduate high school. He worked in a delicatessen all his life. Mom earned a high school diploma, and although sharp as a tack, college was not in the cards for her. I was the first to enter higher education in my family, a classic first-generation, baby boom, community college student. When I arrived at the Miami-Dade Community College North Campus to register, I had no idea what to expect. I was walking into a new land with new language, a new culture and with very different norms that I did not understand. No one at home could help me; they had no basis of understanding.

I was a stranger in a strange land, a border crosser through and through. I am sure I had the same look on my face as the ones I have seen on the majority of the faces who have entered the doors of GCC and community colleges across America. They are the faces of those who cross borders every day. Imagine hearing, seeing, and feeling the message "you belong here" in the moment you cross any border.

A 2019 study by Gopalan and Brady shows that first-generation students and students of color have a higher sense of belonging than their peers at two-year colleges, while at four-year colleges, their sense of belonging is lower than their peers. Belonging can improve a number of outcomes, including academic, health, and engagement. I have witnessed the power of belonging for students, faculty, and staff over the course of my 40 years of service. I have also experienced the impact of belonging and community in my own life as a student and as a professional (Gopalan & Brady, 2020).

I earned my doctorate from the Community College Leadership Program (CCLP) at The University of Texas (UT) at Austin. A hallmark of the program were the presentations to our "block" by community college leaders from around the world. In addition to the challenges, strategies, and campus realities, we learned that there is not a single model of leadership that fits all; authenticity built on a foundation of passionate commitment is the common trait.

Alfredo de Los Santos was one such visiting scholar. He was the vice chancellor of the Maricopa community college system at the time. De Los Santos was an alum of CCLP. Of course, he talked about the work at Maricopa. But it was his personal story, his journey, that impacted our class the most and it is one I will never forget.

Toward the end of his presentation, de Los Santos tearfully shared with us that not only was he the first in his family to earn a PhD, he was also the first in his family to attend college. De Los Santos was also the first Mexican American to earn a PhD from the CCLP at UT. His son, Gerardo, graduated in the class just behind mine, a generation later.

It was customary for our guest speakers to attend a reception after class so that we could meet, greet, and learn from each visitor in a more informal environment. It was a skill that served students well. We all had badges with our names. As I moved down the reception line to greet de Los Santos, I noticed him reading my badge just before we met.

"Hello," I said. "My name is Bob Pura; it is a pleasure to meet you." "Pura," he responded with a clear and distinct Spanish pronunciation. "Pura," I responded, clarifying with a more Anglo Eastern European pronunciation. "Pura," he responded with a smile but now a bit firmer in tone, purposefully exaggerating the Spanish pronunciation, adding "Be proud of who you are." "I am sir," I responded. "My Dad is from Poland."

His booming laughter in response filled the room and was heard by all. Within a week, my classmates had T-shirts made for all in the class with the words "Be Proud of Who You Are!" on the back. De Los Santos was a leader and a role model. He was also a border crosser.

Although Howard Tinberg, professor of English at Bristol Community College in Massachusetts, wrote about community college teachers as "border crossing" in 1993, I first heard the term *border crossers* applied to community college students at the announcement of the Jack Kent Cook Foundation's community college to elite college initiative. Anthony Marx, then president of Amherst College, was the lunchtime speaker at a small half-day gathering of private elite and public community college leaders in DC. He was the first I heard use the term *border crossers* when referring to community college students.

Sandra Kurtinitis (2019), president of the Community College of Baltimore County and past chair of the AACC board, wrote that

> our campuses are microcosms of the communities we serve, living emblems of equity, diversity and inclusion. In our business, diversity must be everybody's business, not just the job of the multicultural affairs office. AACC data show our campuses to be melting pots of color, size and shape. All are welcome, whether wearing a baseball cap, hoodie, hijab or leisure suit. Truly, we are Emma Lazarus's "Give me your tired, your poor," writ large! (p. 1)

More immigrants attend community colleges than any other postsecondary institution. In their article "Immigrants in Community Colleges," Teranishi et al. (2011) state that "immigrant youth and children of immigrants make up a large and increasing share of the nation's population, and over the next few decades they will constitute a significant portion of the U.S. workforce" (p. 153). Increasing access to higher education, as well as their economic and civic engagement, must be a national priority and community colleges are best suited for achieving that objective.

Teranishi et al. understand that community colleges are conveniently located in the communities where the majority of immigrants live and work, are more affordable and create less debt, are open admissions institutions, and accommodate students who work or have family responsibilities. They write that "community colleges are well suited to meet the educational needs of immigrants who want to obtain an affordable postsecondary education, learn English-language skills, and prepare for the labor market" (p. 154).

The Seeds of the Community College

Most look to the Truman Commission as the beginning point of the community college movement, and understandably so. In the first sentence in his letter to commission members with his charge, President Harry Truman (1947) wrote, "As Veterans return to college by the hundreds of thousands, the institutions of higher education face a period of trial which is taxing their resources and their resourcefulness to the utmost." He continues, "Among the more specific questions which I hope the Commission concern itself [with] are ways and means of expanding educational opportunities for all" (Zook, 1947, p. 1).

The commission responded to Truman's charge by developing a six-volume report titled "Higher Education for American Democracy: A Report of the President's Commission on Higher Education," released December 11, 1947. In Volume One, "Establishing the Goals," the Truman Commission selected three main goals for higher education:

- education for a fuller realization of democracy in every phase of living;
- education directly and explicitly for international understanding and cooperation; and
- education for the application of creative imagination and trained intelligence to the solution of social problems and to the administration of public affairs (p. 8).

The commission worked to open the doors to education as wide as the doors to the nation for all:

> It is the responsibility of the community, at the local, State, and National levels, to guarantee that financial barriers do not prevent any able and otherwise qualified young person from receiving the opportunity for higher education. There must be developed in this country the widespread realization that money expended for education is the wisest and soundest of investments in the national interest. The democratic community cannot tolerate a society based upon education for the well-to-do alone. If college opportunities are restricted to those in the higher income brackets, the way is open to the creation and perpetuation of a class society which has no place in the American way of life. (p. 23)

Community colleges today are a reflection of the core values articulated in the 1947 commission, and just as the commission named the report "Higher Education for Democracy," the community colleges of America have earned the distinction of being called "democracy's college." The Truman

Commission report changed the course of higher education in the United States for the better, from "merely being an instrument for producing an intellectual elite" to becoming "the means by which every citizen, youth, and adult, is enabled and encouraged" to pursue higher learning (President's Commission, 1947, p. 101).

Community college historians also point to the founding of Joliet Junior College, near Chicago, Illinois, in 1901 as the first community college. William Rainey Harper, then president of the University of Chicago, and J. Stanley Brown, then principal of Joliet High School, collaborated to found Joliet Junior College in order to expand educational opportunity for public school students and to prepare students for the university. Joliet is the oldest community college that is still in operation.

Benson et al. (2007, 2009, 2017) point to the relationship that existed between President Harper, John Dewey, and Jane Addams. I can't help but wonder what impact those relationships had in the development of Joliet Junior College. Dewey and Harper were friends and colleagues at the University of Chicago. Both were influenced by Jane Addams and the work at Hull House, whose work was to educate women, the working class, and new immigrants providing social skills and civic knowledge needed to impact the community in which they work and live. Each wrote and spoke with clarity and passion about the role of education as a foundation for a more sustainable community and a stronger democracy. It would not be a stretch to suggest that the thumbprints of Addams and Dewey are alongside those of Harper and Brown in the creation of the first junior college in America. President Harper, Jane Addams, and Professor Dewey all possessed the values, vision, and leadership necessary to plant the seeds in America's educational and political soil that grew into the community college movement of today.

The Challenge of Measuring Success

I remember calling the president at Berkshire Community College (BCC), a friend as well as a colleague, after reading the headline in their local newspaper, *The Berkshire Eagle*. It was a front-page, top-of-the-fold comparison of the graduation rates at Williams College and BCC. Williams' graduation rate was about 94% that year, and BCC was about 23% at the time. I called because I knew the president would not be happy. Okay, so I wanted to tease him just a bit as well, but I could tell right from the first hello that this was not a moment for levity. The president was more than a bit grumpy, because the article, (although accurate about the comparative graduation numbers), the headline, and the story did not also compare the differences between an entering Williams college student and a BCC student.

A vice president at Williams once told me that 100% of their next incoming class could have perfect SAT scores. The college chose not to, but the point is made. It is both misleading and problematic to compare outcomes when the input is so dramatically different. While most elite colleges will only admit students from the top fifth percentile of private prep and high school graduating classes, community colleges admit the other 95%.

Hats off to Williams for their graduation rates. Williams is a wonderful college, a pillar of the higher education landscape, an exemplar of excellence at every turn. But the fact that BCC's graduation rate was 23% is also a powerful statement about the impact of the faculty, staff, and students of that college. It would be hard for Williams' students to fail given all their academic preparation, cocurricular and life experiences, economic advantage, family support, and the college's per-student spending. All too often for community college students, however, failure is a reinforcing narrative and an all too familiar lived experience.

The Integrated Postsecondary Education Data System (National Center for Education Data System, 2019) is the nationally required standard by which all institutions of higher education measure graduation rates. According to their website:

> Graduation rate data provide information on institutional productivity and help institutions comply with reporting requirements of the Student Right-to-Know Act and the Higher Education Act, amended. Graduation rates (GR) data are collected for full-time, first-time degree and certificate-seeking undergraduate students. Data collected include:
>
> - number of students entering the institution as full-time, first-time degree or certificate-seeking students in a particular year (cohort), by race/ethnicity and gender;
> - number of students completing their program within a time period equal to one and a half times (150%) the normal period of time, by race/ethnicity, gender, and Pell status; and
> - number of students who transferred to other institutions. (paras. 1–2)

It is most significant that IPEDS measures only first-time, full-time degree-seeking students within 3 years' time. According to the AACC (2019) website data, 37% of community college students attend full-time and 63% part-time. That means that only about one third of community college students could possibly complete their course of study "within one and a half times the normal period of time." A student would be incredibly hard pressed to complete a 60-credit associate degree in that amount of time, attending part-time, working over 20–30 hours a week, and taking care of family. Attending part-time, as two thirds of community college students do, is a socioeconomic reality.

A colleague once said to me that the joy of teaching community college students is that they are in the middle of life and not just preparing for it. That reality is also part of the complexity of measuring success, especially graduation rates. Comparing a college where students are hand selected to ensure success, with an open-door admission's institution, is foolish to say the least, and costly and damaging in far too many regards. That said, IPEDS, as flawed as it is, has value. And as the number of new measuring systems for community college student success increase, Achieving the Dream as one example, the expansion of accurate data provides the opportunity for betterment.

That headline comparing Williams and BCC takes on a different meaning when one looks more closely at some of the most significant variables affecting the success of community college students. Measuring student success at a community college is complex and challenging, so says Thomas Bailey, current president of Teachers College at Columbia and former director of the CCRC. In 2005 he wrote:

> Overall, compared with students at baccalaureate institutions, community college students have more characteristics that might compromise their ability to succeed in college. They have generally lower test scores in high school and are far more likely to delay enrollment in college after high school, attend part time, or interrupt their college studies. Also, they are much more likely to come from households in the lower SES quartiles. All of these factors have been shown in many studies to be related to lower retention and graduation. Finally, community colleges serve many older students who face additional challenges to educational success because they are more likely to work full-time and may have families to support—characteristics that have been found to be significant barriers to educational success. (p. 2)

Researchers at North Carolina State University designed the Revealing Institutional Strengths and Challenges survey. They surveyed nearly 6,000 two-year college students from 10 community colleges in California, Michigan, Nebraska, North Carolina, South Dakota, Texas, Virginia, Wisconsin, and Wyoming in fall 2017 and 2018. The survey found that working and paying for expenses were the top two challenges community college students said impeded their academic success. About 2,100 students said work was the largest challenge they faced, with 61% saying the number of hours they worked didn't leave them enough time to study. About 50% of students reported their wages didn't cover their expenses.

Students also reported difficulty paying for living expenses, textbooks, tuition, and childcare. Thirty percent of students reported difficulty balancing familial responsibilities with college, dealing with family members' and friends' health problems, and finding childcare. Among those who cited these personal problems, 11% said their family did not support them going to college.

The very troubling and sad truth about education today is that from pre-K through higher education, the socioeconomic status of students is still the most significant predictor of success, and money-related issues remain among the largest challenges. When announcing the war on poverty, President Lyndon B. Johnson (1964) said, "Unfortunately, many Americans live on the outskirts of hope, some because of their poverty, and some because of their color, and all too many because of both" (para. 18).

Far too many Americans still live on the outskirts of hope. Our nation must do better, and community colleges are essential partners toward that end.

On Access, Alienation, and Outcomes

Opening the doors to education for all who aspire to a better life, while maintaining high academic standards, is the most noble mission in all of higher education. But what if those doors were to close? What if access was denied? What if a clear and affordable path to a college education was not available to all? A colleague at GCC once said, "If nearby Amherst or Williams Colleges were to close, each of those students would find another place for their education. But if GCC were to close, where would our students go?" What would come of those denied access on that frigate we call education, whose dreams were now deferred?

In 1951 sociologist Robert Merton wrote that anomie, alienation, or normlessness will occur if there is an acute disjuncture between society's accepted goals and the legitimate means available to achieve them. Crime, mental health issues, addiction, and deviant behavior are predictable outcomes; alienation is inevitable. He added that American culture "appears to approximate the polar types in which great emphasis upon certain goals occurs without equivalent emphasis upon institutional means" (p. 136): housing, health care, social and economic mobility—the proverbial American Dream. He adds that equal access to the means to achieve those goals, such as access to a good education and a good job with family-sustaining wages, is not available to all. That anomic outcome inevitably divides a nation between those with access to opportunity and those without. The diploma divide widens, increasing the binary nature of our society. The foundation of our democracy is then weakened as a result (Merton, 1951).

In an article published in *The Hill*, Wilson (2017) writes that "the differences between those who have attained a college degree and those who have not is driving changes in the way people are living their lives, from the decision to get married to our views of the world" (para. 5). The diploma divide is changing our political environment, some suggesting that our democracy is failing as a result. The increasing divide between urban and rural communities, as well as between younger and older Americans, is also most evident in the increasingly binary experiences of those who are prepared for economic success with a college degree in hand and those who are not.

More Americans are going to college today than ever before. Almost 60% of recent high school graduates are attending college, according to the National Center for Education Statistics (2010). Over 50% of America's high school graduates did not attend college in 1970. By 2020 a third of those 25–29 years old and almost 40% of women in that age group completed a four-year degree (Wilson, 2017).

More students are also graduating with more debt than ever. The nation's resolve with regard to that debt still in debate. That debt load has risen to around $864 billion as of 2020. That investment and that debt load, however, can pay off. As the economy demands higher levels of education for more skilled jobs, even in the manufacturing sector, the difference between what a college graduate can expect to earn over a lifetime and what a high school graduate will make has never been greater. We have made it far too difficult for a person with only a high school diploma to gain access to a good job at good wages, and current projections suggest that it will only get more challenging. Thirty-five percent of job openings will require a bachelor's degree, 30% will require an associate degree, and about 36% will require at least a high school diploma (Wilson, 2017).

Today, the median annual earnings of a person who has earned a college degree and is working full-time is approximately $50,000. Median earnings of those with a high school education are just $30,000, according to Richard Fry, a labor economist at the Pew Research Center. That $20,000 gap is larger today than the gap between members of the previous generation. The baby boom generation entered the workforce with far more opportunities for lower-skilled jobs than millennials have today (Wilson, 2017).

It is also interesting that, as opposed to earlier generations, those without a college degree are less likely to be married than those who have a degree. They are more likely to use tobacco and abuse illegal drugs according to a national survey conducted by the Substance Abuse and Mental Health Services Administration (Wilson, 2017).

Those without a college degree are expressing more dissatisfaction with life. Nearly three quarters of those without a college degree say most other people cannot be trusted, while just 41% of those who are college educated say the same, according to the General Social Survey. More than 50% of those without a college education say they find life routine, while 62% of those with a college degree call life exciting (Wilson, 2017).

Princeton University economists Anne Case and Angus Deaton have found a marked rise in mortality rates, in particular among white Americans without a college degree. At the same time, mortality rates have fallen for every other cohort in American society. Mortality rates for noncollege-educated whites were 30% higher than among African Americans of any education level. Americans without a college degree are seemingly experiencing economic hopelessness in dramatically new ways. The diploma divide is killing us (Case & Deaton, 2015).

Research now also shows that college graduates were less likely to lose their job during the coronavirus pandemic than those without a degree according to the COVID Inequality Project (Adams et al., 2021). The CIP is a project interested in understanding how the pandemic and government policies impacted inequality. The project surveyed nearly 17,000 people in the United States and United Kingdom and found that college graduates were eight percentage points less likely to lose their job due to the economic fallout from COVID-19 than workers without a college degree. In the United Kingdom, the gap was six percentage points. College graduates were also less likely to experience income losses. The research suggested this outcome could be related to the kinds of jobs college graduates hold. Although not surprising given the social distancing measures, the study found that the likelihood of losing your job was related to being able to work from home. Workers in the United States who could perform all of their job from home were 33 percentage points less likely to have lost their job than those who could perform none of their job at home (Whistle, 2020).

According to David Brooks in his February 18, 2019, opinion piece in *The New York Times*, social isolation is a problem underlying our nation's most significant social problems. In response, The Aspen Institute developed Weave: The Social Fabric Project. They point out that the problem is being solved by people around the country, at the local level, every day who are building community and weaving the social fabric. Community colleges are found at the very center of those communities, over 100 years after John Dewey spoke of the need for education at the center of community.

There are over 1,100 community colleges in the urban, suburban, and rural communities of our nation. The individual, along with the collective, impact of those colleges is a powerful and profound statement about access, excellence, and the sustainability of community. As go colleges in the community, so goes the community; as go those communities, so goes our nation.

Reflections

Bob began this chapter with a discussion of his own identity and positionality. It is equally important for me to do the same. Unlike Bob, I never attended a community college, though my high school guidance counselor recommended that I enroll in one and then "try" to transfer to a four-year college. I was a Black girl in a white private high school, and this was only the second time the guidance counselor met with me. He really knew nothing about me at all. A year or two before our college counseling meeting, he suggested I enroll in the "non-Regents" courses because they were "the same as the Regents courses but had less homework." I was 14 and a sophomore in high school. Less homework sounded good to me. I didn't realize at the time that taking the non-Regents courses would lead to a non-Regents diploma, which would make me less competitive for four-year colleges. He raised this point to me during our one and only college counseling meeting and used the fact that I wouldn't have a Regents diploma as the rationale for me not pursuing a four-year college. He didn't mention his role in encouraging me to take the non-Regents courses; instead he assumed I wasn't capable. When I graduated from high school, community colleges held a negative stigma in my view, so I only applied to four-year colleges.

Both of my parents have bachelor's degrees from Historically Black Colleges and Universities (HBCUs). Like community colleges, HBCUs provide access to those other institutions exclude. Given that my parents put all four of their children through 12 years of private education, it was always assumed I would go to college (just as it was expected of my mother even though she was the first in her family to go to college). It was also expected of my dad, if he wanted to marry my mom. She made that very clear.

Although I was a second-generation college student and the youngest of four children, my parents and I didn't talk much (if at all) about how or where I would go to school, but we all knew I was going to get my baccalaureate degree. My sister and I are the only two of my parents' children who graduated from college. My parents did some postbaccalaureate work at Columbia University, and I am the only person in my immediate and extended family to earn a PhD.

My decision to seek a doctorate came after working in student affairs for several years and repeatedly seeing Black and Brown students who looked like me experience a negative campus racial climate that reflected the systemic racism in larger society. Their experiences also mirrored my own as I often felt isolated during most of my college years on a predominantly white campus. My friends and I, most of whom were students of color, had to find and create our own sense of belonging through our own organizations like the Black Student Union, El Arco Iris Latino, and my beloved Delta Sigma Theta.

As I pursued my PhD, I became interested in the ways institutional and state policy impacted the experiences of students of color. Although I never attended a community college, they were always an interest of mine, because of my own racialized experiences in high school and college. My guidance counselor recommended that I go to a community college, and if I listened, I likely would have required remedial courses, given that Black students are more likely to enroll in remediation; and community college students are more likely to require remediation, even after controlling for academic preparedness (Attewell et al., 2006). These findings may provide clues to why community colleges, despite their welcoming reputation, may not be the first choice for some students.

The negative stigma of community colleges is something we in higher education must continue to grapple with if we are to increase college enrollment and educational attainment. My experience with my high school guidance counselor was not unique, and I am sure his recommendation to me was based not just in racial and gender bias but also in bias against two-year colleges. And as clever as the hashtag #EndCCStigma[1] is, a social media campaign is not enough to eliminate this deeply rooted stigma.

Between 2010 and 2017, enrollment in community colleges declined by 14.4%. When looking at the period between 2001 and 2017, a notable shift in demographics becomes clear. White enrollment in community colleges dropped from 60% in 2001 to 46% in 2017. During the same period, enrollment for students of color increased from 40% to approximately 53% but has remained relatively steady between 2013 and 2017 (AACC, 2019). Overall, community college enrollment has continued to decline since 2017, and the decline appears to be worsening, as enrollment dropped by 1.7% in 2017 and by 3.4% in spring 2019 (Fain, 2019).

The diversity of community colleges, however, is not likely to change, given the past 20-year trends and the increasing racial/ethnic diversity of communities across the country. While community colleges are open to all, institutional leaders must consider the success of students who are racially, ethnically, and linguistically diverse. In other words, students who enroll in community colleges must be able to expect that they will reach their goals and potentially develop new ones. Indeed, community colleges are expected to virtually be all things to all people. States and local communities look to them to increase workforce and rural/urban development. Students look to transfer, earn a baccalaureate degree, obtain skills for work, and/or improve their academic skills. Approximately 80% of students who enter a community college seek a four-year college degree or higher; however, only 30% of students who started at a community college in 2012 transferred, and only 13% went on to earn a bachelor degree within 6 years (Shapiro et al., 2017). Further, rates for students from lower-income backgrounds or who are Black or Latinx are even lower. For community colleges to truly maintain their role as democracy's colleges, they must improve these outcomes. Providing access is only one step toward this goal.

As Bob rightfully notes in this chapter, it is foolish to compare graduation rates of open access two-year colleges with highly selective four-year colleges and universities. At the same time, community colleges must recognize degree completion and transfer rates are not where they need to be. Students who arrive at the doorstep of two-year institutions often arrive with more challenges that hinder their success than their four-year counterparts. And still most of them seek a bachelor's degree. Institutional leaders' cannot use these challenges as a rationale for not getting more students to achieve their goals. As we indicate in this chapter, individual lives and community vitality depend on community colleges to advance access *and* equity.

Discussion Questions

1. How do your social and professional identities shape who you are as a practitioner, policymaker, or leader? How often do you reflect on your identity and the ways it impacts your perspective and leadership?
2. What are the strengths and challenges of maintaining a comprehensive community college mission?
3. How should community colleges be evaluated on success? How should success be defined for students, faculty, and the state?
4. What responsibility does community college leadership have in addressing low transfer and baccalaureate rates of students who begin

their academic careers at a community college? What other factors should be considered when presenting and monitoring transfer, credential, and degree completion rates?

5. In what ways might institutional leaders maintain access and promote equity in terms of enrollment, student success, transfer, and degree completion?

Note

1. In February 2019, Owens Community College President Steve Robinson started a social media campaign to end the stigma that is often associated with community colleges by broadening awareness of the importance of community colleges, particularly during a time when many two-year institutions are removing "community" from their college name.

3

THE COMMUNITY'S COLLEGE

There is no power for change greater than a community discovering what it cares about.

—Margaret J. Wheatley

Walking through the Stop & Shop on High Street in Greenfield was as much a part of my work as president of GCC as it was a weekly function of hunting and gathering. The interactions and discussions, whether they occurred in frozen foods, dairy, or at check out, were always helpful in connecting the college and the community. People appreciated my time, the access, and the relationship. I understood that responsibility to the community, and to be honest, I enjoyed it. It wasn't a strategy; it was a way of being. That is what made it authentic. I wouldn't recommend taking a presidency at a small rural community college unless you are authentically committed to being a part of and committed to building community on and off campus. Community college leaders must be as active and engaged walking the streets and grocery aisles of the community as they are walking the halls of the campus.

In the seminal 1988 AACC publication, "Building Communities: A Vision on the Future of Community Colleges," the authors wrote

> We propose, therefore, that the theme "Building Communities" become the new rallying point for the community college in America. We define the term "community" not only as a region to be served, but also as a climate to be created. (p. 7)

Over the course of my 40-year career, I have learned that the internal community of a college and the community to be served are inexorably linked. Building a community environment on a campus is as important to the sustainability of the community it serves as it is to the sustainability of the college. Without that reservoir on which to draw from, the external effort is rendered shallow. Both college and community are then less likely to reach their full potential. The foundations of our democracy are then weakened as a result.

Building a Climate of Community on Campus

Although born in Queens, I grew up in the southernmost tip of New York: Miami, Florida. We lived at 1236 Drexel Avenue, apartment 2, in what is now known as South Beach, for my first 2 years of school. Each morning I would walk along Washington Avenue, the commerce center of the area, to Central Beach Elementary School just a few blocks away. My mom, dad, uncle, and grandfather were already at work at the grocery store. As I walked along that route, Mom would stand in front of the store making sure I was okay. And so did the owner of the corner drug store, the butcher, and the woman from the candy store. They all watched out for me, as if I was their own. My understanding about community started on that walk to school with everyone watching out for me as if I was one of their own kids—*as if I was one of their own.* I was getting my first lesson in building and sustaining community.

In his book, *Our Kids*, Harvard Professor Robert Putnam (2015) writes eloquently about the state of upward mobility in the United States. By looking back at his hometown in 1950s Ohio compared with today, he describes how widening income gaps have brought profound but negative changes to families, neighborhoods, and schools in ways that give big advantages to children at the top and make it ever harder for those below to work their way up. Putnam demonstrated with solid data that when communities embrace all children "as our own," no matter the class, race, or religion, children have stronger foundations on which to build. Democracy is then on more solid footing. As we have proposed, without strong communities our nation is built on a house of cards.

Relationships matter on community college campuses; so too does the authentic feeling of belonging to a community. Learning and student success are then more achievable. It is an environment that is created at GCC and so many community colleges across the nation, each college modeling the community it wants the nation to become. Belonging and community are all too often first-time experiences for all too many community college students. Here are just a few examples of how and where those outcomes are accomplished.

The GCC Math Studio

Soon after arriving at GCC as its ninth president, I received a phone call from the chair of the math department: "We would like to transform the conference room in the center of our offices into a studio for math students. They went on to say "We want them to have a space near our offices where they can work together solving math problems. They would help each other learn and we will be always around the studio. There will be no waiting to make an appointment." So that is exactly what we did: We transformed the space, and students came.

According to the GCC (2019) website,

> The Math Studio strives to be a community of math learners where students are encouraged to drop in to work with other students in mathematics. The Math Studio is staffed by math faculty members throughout the week. We work not just with students in math classes but also with students in classes that have math components to them (examples include economics, chemistry, etc.). (para. 1)

A few months after the opening of the math studio, I received a call from security. It was Friday evening at 5:00 p.m. "Dr. Pura, we have a problem." No college president wants a call from security on a Friday evening that starts this way. "What's the problem," I asked. The officer paused. "Well sir, there are students in the math studio; it is scheduled to close at 5:00 p.m., but they don't want to leave. They just ordered pizza so that they can all study for a test on Monday." I think I actually laughed right out loud. "Those are the problems we want!" I am not sure how well they all did on those exams, but I am 100% certain of the transformational impact of their collective experience in that studio, together.

In a short period of time, the chair of the business department came to my office and said, "Hey, Mr. President, we want one of those!" Science and humanities soon followed. All the studios were paid for with private community dollars. Those business leaders in small, rural Franklin County understood the importance of that kind of space. Building community was not a strategic initiative at GCC; it was a reflection of a core college value.

The library; the advising, fitness, student life, and peer tutoring centers; the art, music, and academic studios, along with the dining commons, were some of the spaces that relationships and community were developed. Students felt they had a place and space that they belonged. They worked together, solved problems together, learned together, and built community together. That math studio, and those that followed, were microcosms of the larger college culture.

When visitors toured the campus many would talk about the beauty of the building design or the student art that hung on the walls. However, when educators toured the campus, it was the studios they were interested in most. Those educators understood and respected the power of community in a learning environment.

The importance of creating community for students, faculty, and staff was an authentic core value of GCC and its culture. More than the success of any one program, any one initiative, or any one academic department, it was the climate of community as an authentic component of the college's culture that was the foundation of all its success.

On the Importance of Gathering as Community

In *Teaching to Transgress: Education as the Practice of Freedom*, bell hooks (1994) wrote, "As a classroom community, our capacity to generate excitement is deeply affected by our interest in one another, in hearing one another's voices, in recognizing one another's presence" (p. 8). The respectful relationships described by hooks were found in the studios of GCC, and we worked to establish that same principle and create that environment at our all-college meetings. It was important to be explicit about "our interest in one another, in hearing one another's voices, in recognizing one another's presence."

Every month at GCC, I met with the college community at what we called "all-college" meetings. All faculty, staff, and students were invited. It was not a mandatory meeting, yet attendance was pretty strong over the course of those 18 years. I held monthly meetings with all faculty at BCC as chief academic officer (CAO), so when I came to Greenfield and found those all-college meetings were already a part of the college culture, I was thrilled. Those meetings were an important opportunity for communicating, decision-making, and especially community building. I enjoyed preparing for that meeting as much as I did preparing for a class when I taught years earlier at Massasoit Community College in Brockton, Massachusetts. I started each meeting with music as folks were walking in and getting seated. On occasion, one or two members of the faculty or staff even danced into the lecture hall.

Through college faculty and staff, I invited students from around GCC to "share their voice" at the final meeting of the academic year. It was great fun and was uplifting to take the moment to celebrate our students' voice and their achievements; sometimes it was dance, poetry, science, art, nursing, or music; every voice was important. I remember when the Accounting Club students were introduced and received a standing ovation for their work, providing free tax preparation for seniors in the community.

The faculty and staff in attendance understood the importance of the standing ovations for each of those students recognized and to the culture of the college. In recognizing and celebrating our students' voices, we were also recognizing and celebrating the good work of the faculty, staff, and college. GCC faculty and staff beamed with pride, as if those students were their own kids.

Those all-college meetings provided the opportunity to raise and discuss the issues that challenged us from governance to teaching and learning. Some of those meetings were fun and celebratory, and some were filled with the angst and the sausage making of any community while we discussed its challenges. (Sausage making is often referred to as the complex process of communication/decision-making within a democracy or shared governance system). We talked about state or community concerns, and we looked into our finances together. We came together in the aftermath of national or international tragedies, and we came together to celebrate our college data and achievements. At the first meeting of the academic year, we always took the time to introduce all new employees. It was at that first meeting that I had the opportunity to welcome folks to the start of a new academic year, setting the tone and direction. What a great opportunity for any leader.

The GCC Food Pantry

I remember one particular all-college meeting when a member of the faculty raised her hand and said, "We put snacks out every once in a while for students in the studio adjacent to our department offices. It is gone in like 30 seconds. I am curious, is anyone else having that same experience (putting out food, and then it's gone pretty quickly)?" "Yes," said another faculty member. "We put peanut butter and crackers out, and it's gone within an hour or two," said yet another member of the college community. Then another.

That conversation ultimately led to the creation of the GCC Food Pantry. The abundance of research and the recognition of food insecurity as a national collegiate concern was a year or 3 away. GCC was, at the time, the second community college in the nation and the first east of the Mississippi to recognize and address student hunger by creating a food pantry on campus.

The data today with regard to food insecurity is stark. "Struggling to Survive, Striving to Succeed: Food and Housing Insecurities in the Community College" (Wood et al., 2017), a study that surveyed 3,647 California community college students, reported that insecurities were more common with students of color (especially Black men) and had widespread educational consequences, including a greater likelihood of dropping out. Another study,

"Hunger on Campus," added that insecurities were also more common among community college and first-generation students and caused students to skip classes, withdraw from courses, or opt out of buying required textbooks. That study also reported that 50% of community college students and 47% of four-year college students reported food insecurity. Twenty-five percent and 20% (respectively) had very low food security. At community colleges, "13 percent of all respondents (regardless of food insecurity) experienced homelessness, compared to 7 percent at four-year schools" (The National Student Campaign Against Hunger and Homelessness, 2016, p. 7). Hunger on Campus also found that programs such as campus meal plans, Pell grants, student loans, and the Supplemental Nutrition Assistance Program (SNAP) have not been completely effective in eliminating food insecurity (Association of American Colleges and Universities [AAC&U] News, 2017).

I am not aware of any college today that has not responded to the tragic reality of food insecurity. That is both the bad and good news. As was said at that GCC all-college meeting, "It's hard to learn when you are hungry."

Above all else, those all-college meetings gave our college the opportunity to come together as a community, to talk, to celebrate, on occasion to fight, but always to build and sustain the college community. Creating an environment on campus that modeled community for all students is as lasting and as meaningful as the skills needed for employment.

Of all the wonderful comments I have heard from alumni over the years about their favorite faculty or staff at GCC, it was the relationships, the feeling of belonging, and sense of community that I heard about most consistently. For all too many, it was an experience the first of its kind.

Meeting the Needs of a Changing Student Body

Another hallmark of the community college has been its ability to adjust quickly to change. They turn on a dime, often without having that dime. One such area of change has been, and is increasingly so, the broad age range of community college students.

Most colleges and universities admit the "traditional" 18-year-old. According to the AACC, the average age of the community college student in 2021 was a "nontraditional" 28 years of age. It is imperative that community colleges continue to adjust and evolve to meet the changing demographics of the community it serves. It is important to the relationship between college and community. It is also in the self-preserving interest of the college (AACC, 2021).

I had known Ethel (Risky) Case, dean of continuing education at GCC, over the course of my years serving the commonwealth, but she retired before

I arrived as president. Risky was the name all referred to her as, and few have been more appropriately named. The pipe-smoking Brooklyn native was too aggressive and brash to some, wonderfully bold to others. She was admired and respected by most. I loved her. She welcomed me into the college and community with open arms and heart. That was a good thing.

Early on in my tenure, at one particular college function at my house, Risky cornered me, looked me dead in the eye, pointed her finger, and said, "Robert, here is what you need to do." I wasn't offended by her getting in my face or the boldness of her approach. In fact, I think I might have chuckled in light of the fact that it was Risky after all. It is not an approach that I would recommend to any developing leader, but it sure did work for Risky.

In that discussion she talked about the changing demographics, the aging of the community. She explained to me that more and more people were retiring but had great interest in continuing their learning. The idea of serving the intellectual needs of those folks was appealing to me, and the data bore her out.

After a few conversations with the leadership team of the college and in particular the dean of community education, the GCC Senior Symposia was born. Because of the leadership and commitment of that dean, Risky, and a handful of retired leaders, the Senior Symposium was a rather significant success.

Self-governance, curriculum, and a fiscal model were developed that empowered and gave ownership to those involved. It was leadership of that dean and the relationships built in that group that created a community that continues to this day. An article in the Springfield newspaper described the Symposia:

> Loren W. Kramer looks forward to each of Greenfield Community College's new semesters. He has learned about music, history, geology, the environment and politics. But he's not a traditional community college student: The 76-year-old is a regular attendee at the Senior Symposia Program. (Urban, 2019, para. 1)

For the past 5 or 6 years he has attended a half dozen programs per semester. "The mainstream media doesn't do really well with providing a broad variety of information about things that affect us in this country," he said. "So, I'm always looking for some other source."

> The Senior Symposia Program at Greenfield Community College is a collaborative effort between Greenfield Community College and area senior citizens to provide a way for seniors to continue their education in a format that best suits their needs, interests and resources.

In existence since 2003, "the program is by (seniors) and for (seniors)," said Robert J. Barba, dean for community education. Persons, age 50 and older, are encouraged to attend.

"I'm impressed with the diversity and quality of the presentations," Kramer said. "They choose subjects—partly suggested by participants—from a wide spectrum of interest, and they are always of real importance for our local area as well as the nation."

The symposia make education accessible to seniors and is planned and run by a volunteer board of seniors with support from the college. "People on the board are well connected and know some pretty astonishingly talented people and get them to teach for us," Barba said.

"We have a wealth of good presenters in the valley here," Kramer said. "We are lucky to have such quality presentations."

Attendance at the sessions at the community college's downtown center at 270 Main St. averages about 50, an increase over earlier years. Barba attributed the increase in participation to the "really excellent," affordable classes.

The cost for all symposia is $10 per two-hour symposium. Financial assistance is available by pre-registration only. There is no financial assistance available for same-day registration, but guest passes are available for first-time attendees. (Urban, 2019, paras. 7–8)

At the younger age range of issues at the social center of a community are students in area high schools. In addition to responding to the needs of an aging population, community colleges are also responding to the needs of area high school students, while they are still attending high school. Because of financial, academic, or social issues, many high school students are ready for a change. That need for a change is often met by attending a community college. Those enrolled in dual enrollment or early college programs are often students who

- wanted to take a course at the college not offered at the high school;
- did not feel that they "fit in" the high school and were "at risk" of failing out; or
- wanted to attend the college their senior year, getting credit at both.

Known as dual enrollment, early college, or whatever the local college chooses as its name, those programs have become significant to colleges, communities, students, and their families.

GCC had started a program for students at risk of failing and dropping out at Amherst High School a few years before I arrived. Each year, counselors at the high school would recommend students who they felt were academically capable but who were not fitting into the high school environment. The high school, family, and the college all contributed to the funding of the program. Attending the graduation dinners was a very moving experience. A student and a parent would speak. I was not the only one in the room moved to tears. "This saved my daughter's life, literally," said one parent. "She would be dead from drugs if it were not for GCC and this program." A student speaker one year talked about how she had dropped out and was living on the streets. She graduated GCC and had just received a full scholarship to a college in Vermont.

A few years later, with funds from a community donor, we broadened that program to another high school with similar results: a 98% graduation rate. The shift from dropping out to college graduate was powerful for all involved.

Today, dual enrollment and early college programs are significant to the work of community colleges. Early college opens the community colleges' doors to high school students who can earn a high school diploma and an associate degree or 2 years of college credits at the same time. Those programs have a positive, lasting impact on participants' enrollment and success in college, according to a policy brief, "The Lasting Benefits and Strong Returns of Early College High Schools," from the American Institutes of Research (2020). The research also found a strong return on investments made by the colleges.

One study found that 84% of early college students then enrolled in college, compared with 77% of their peers in a control group. And early college students are more likely than their peers to earn a college degree, with 21% of participants in one study graduating with a bachelor's degree within 4 years compared to 11% of control group students. Within 6 years, the gap closed to 30% for early college participants and 25% for their peers. Another study found an average increase of $33,709 in lifetime earnings for early-college participants.

Building a Bridge Between Community and College

Another wonderful example of the importance of building a bridge between the college and the broader community was the GCC student art show. I enjoyed that evening a great deal.

Leo Hwang, dean of humanities, wrote the following in an email to me describing what that art show means for college and community:

> For me, the Student Art Show is the embodiment of our work as educators. How do we imagine the greatest capacities of community colleges? Capacity where we desire for our students the unveiling of possibilities that

are unbounded by class, background, race, gender, disabilities? In the Art Department at Greenfield Community College, faculty work with students in ways that transcend privilege. At GCC the opportunity is not something nurtured from childhood, but something that is present now. The opportunity is in the attention faculty give their students, the high expectations, and structured support that allows a student to see beyond their current capacity and, sometimes to a shocking degree, discover what they are capable of. Isn't that the mission, the dream of all community college faculty?

In our society, art education is often reserved only for those with wealth or the social capital to spend on art classes, art supplies, and art schools. But at Greenfield Community College there is access to incredible faculty who are willing to work with anyone who has the desire to learn and grow as an artist. Sometimes in fits and starts, sometimes in torrents, students grow and document that growth in their portfolios. Nowhere is that more evident than in the Student Art Show.

More than just a celebration of the work students in the Art program have accomplished over the year, the Student Art Show is a curricular assessment tool that the department collectively uses to ascertain whether the student work that is coming out of their classes is meeting the course objectives and expectations. If the work is not meeting expectations, it is an opportunity to revise curriculum, work with peers on pedagogy, and to rethink how programs are constructed. The Student Art Show is a physical manifestation of how great curriculum redesign is supposed to happen.

And then, the Student Art Show is also a gala celebration of everything the Art Department has produced with their students over the course of the year. It is an opportunity for the community to see what their sons and daughters, husbands and wives, friends and neighbors have been doing in all those long hours in the studios. Unlike perhaps any other event at Greenfield Community College, it is the night that every square foot of that wing of the building is traversed by hundreds of visitors so that at times there is barely enough room to pass by a painting without accidentally jostling another visitor, which inevitably leads to chance encounters with friends and acquaintances from around the county. I like to talk about how my plumber, chiropractor, nurse, and auto mechanic are all GCC alumni. Similarly, at the Student Art Show, you bump into your neighbors, your waiter, the editor for the local newspaper, the parents of your child's best friend; all manners of people peruse the halls in various states of awe and amazement.

The event itself is exhausting for the faculty. But it is also a gift from the faculty to the students. What better way to demonstrate their respect, encouragement, and love for the students than to honor them in the Student Art Show. These students and these pieces of work have been deemed the best representation of what Greenfield Community College students can do, how can that be anything except joyful. (Personal communication, February 20, 2019)

GCC opened its doors to many community partners and hosted many community activities. Examples include the MLK Day community events, Chamber of Commerce breakfasts, youth soccer, the United Way Art Auction, the Green River Music and Balloon Festival, the YMCA Young Leaders Club, Blue Cross Blood Drives, the Greenfield High School/YMCA/ GCC Intergenerational Dance, Changing Lives Through Literature, the Nolumbeka Project: A Native American Dance, political presentations/ debates, and community conversations, just to name a few. I can't think of a community college in America that does not have its own long list of community-based activities. Each year and at each college, community colleges are making good on Dewey's concept of the school as the social center of a community.

Civic engagement must be modeled by more than the college president. The faculty and staff of GCC embraced that responsibility, not as a strategy, but as an authentic lifestyle for those folks. The relationship between college and community is enhanced by the number of faculty and staff actively engaged in local organizations. Eighty-three percent of the 320 faculty and staff live in the community they serve and volunteer at over 150 community-based locations.

Hosting community events, opening the college doors to music and the arts, and convening community conversations along with faculty/staff civic engagement are examples of activities that help build the relationship between college and community, creating the community's college.

Meeting the Need for an Educated Workforce

I sat on the chamber of commerce board pretty much the entire time I worked at GCC, taking my turn as chair. I also served on the hospital, arts, and regional employment boards, among many others. The intention was to serve community, and it was most beneficial to the college. It is essential for colleges to link their academic programs with local community workforce needs. Serving on those boards was beneficial toward that end.

The Truman Commission wrote, "Higher education must inspire its graduates with high social aims as well as endow them with specialized information and technical skill. Teaching and learning must be invested with public purpose" (President's Commission on Higher Education, 1947, p. 61). With great clarity they wrote of "the Unity of Education," declaring that education "develops in the student the qualities of mind and personality required of him both for making a living and building a life" (p. 62). The commission adds with emphasis that "it is urgently important in American education today that the age-old distinction between education for living and education for making a living be discarded" (p. 62).

The commission articulated the need to provide career-relevant education and training within the purpose and goals of a college degree:

> To build a richly textured and gracious life is a good and desirable purpose, but few of us can make such a life without first making a living. Cultural values soon take wing when men cannot get and hold jobs. (p. 62)

The comprehensive mission of the community college builds pathways for transfer with four-year college partners and workforce-specific programs in partnership with local business and industry. Employable skills and a liberal arts core are not at odds with one another; rather, together they speak to the future of work. The same can be said for the joining of the long-term aspirations of students alongside their more immediate need for employment. I have never met a student who didn't want a good job as a result of a college degree, and I'm not aware of a community college that does not want to work closely with local business and industry to build the educated workforce needed for local economic development. The unity of education's purposes embrace "branches from the same tree" as Einstein wrote in 1937 (Bear & Skorton, 2018, p. 2).

I remember driving back from a radio talk show about developing the local workforce with the director of the Regional Employment Board (REB). As panelists we both talked about partnerships, strengths in the community, and demanding needs. "Why aren't I on your board?" she asked. "It would enhance our work together even more," she added. "Good question," I responded. "Let's change that." And we did. She became a member of the board of trustees not long after that conversation. She served the college and community extremely well, better integrating the college/community workforce agenda. Local college and community boards have that potential. It paid off in quick time.

Soon after that ride and her appointment, the chief executive officer (CEO) of a local manufacturing company and a local business leader wanted to see more being done to develop a workforce pipeline for manufacturing. He met and talked with the REB director, the leadership of Franklin County Tech (FCT) High School, our leadership team at GCC, the mayor, and local state representatives. Those relationships between agencies and their leadership are important.

Based on the outcome of those conversations, the CEO of that company raised $250,000 from local manufacturers and then motivated the state legislative delegation to match it. With that support and commitment, a $500,000 state-of-the-art manufacturing class/lab was built at FCT. A high school/college/REB/private industry partnership was created, serving both students and community. Together we developed curriculum and internships, students got jobs, and manufacturers got the needed pipeline. I often said we did more with less in our community, and this is another example of the power of that collaboration. But I would always add, "It would be great if, every once in a while, we had more to do more."

The Northern Tier Project

Congressman John Olver called on GCC to work with him and community leaders in 2005 on what he had labeled "The Northern Tier Project." The northern tier was a stretch of Massachusetts in our service region, high on all poverty indicators, yet all too invisible. The congressman wanted to move the economic development needles throughout Franklin County. At the initial meetings, clusters were formed, bringing together key stakeholders in health care, education, the creative economy, outdoor recreation, the green economy, agriculture, and manufacturing. Each cluster was a small yet significant part of the economy of the region. GCC was seated front and center in each.

The congressman convened the conversation, pointed us in a direction, and then backed up the project with grants to support the work each group had designed. Those clusters opened doors, built relationships, created new programs, and convened organizational and strategic meetings, and resources were found and allocated. The community looked to strengthen its economic foundations, and GCC was at the heart of it. I learned a great deal from Congressman Olver about leadership and community action. At one of his many retirement parties, I said, "Many elected officials go off to Washington with good intentions, only to fight windmills. Our congressman, in his passion regarding climate change, went to DC and built them." John Olver lived the words of Speaker Tip O'Neill who infamously said that "all politics are local." Community college leaders have long understood that not only are all politics local, but so too is education.

A Voice in the Community

The president of the community's college has many different opportunities for leadership in the community. From joining local civic groups, like the Rotary and chamber of commerce, to participation in town committees and boards, each is an opportunity to strengthen the relationship between town and gown, between community and college.

The so-called bully pulpit of leadership is real. I enjoyed the spoken word. Talking with students at orientation and faculty and staff at monthly meetings and speaking at commencement was an honor and privilege. I felt the same about every opportunity for public speaking in the community. If they invited me, I showed up!

I also enjoyed the written word. Sending "all user" emails to the college community during challenging times was important. It was just as important for the community to hear from all local leaders in those moments, including the local college president. Taking the time to write op-ed pieces is important; it is also a responsibility. I enjoyed those opportunities for communicating to and with the broader community. It is a key to the link between college and community and an essential contribution to the strengthening of democracy at the local community level.

Developing a good relationship with the editors and reporters who cover the college was important. The more local the paper the more important the relationship between the college and the newspaper. The *Greenfield Recorder* is a wonderful local paper covering community news, and they also help to create community. The editors get that, so do each of the reporters; their photographer captures the community in images as the writers do in words. They are able to balance the dual mission of reporting about the community as well as building community. Such is the challenge of a small, rural newspaper. It is not all that easy, especially because they also have to generate revenue.

Respecting their mission, their work, and their challenges built the same respect for our work and our challenges. I always responded to their calls, always told them the truth, and also told them when I could not respond. In return, I always felt they were honest and fair with their reporting. They have a responsibility to the community, as do we. I found the same to be true with the radio, television, and the local cable media. Building trust with all in the media is important. That relationship serves college, community, and news professionals well.

Holding the door to higher education open, like lighting the lamp of lady liberty, is simply not enough in and of itself to equip students with the skills and knowledge necessary to succeed. Providing access to a college education, even if it is located in the community, is not enough to build an economy, sustain the community, or anchor our democracy. Leadership matters.

Reflections

In this chapter Bob shares ways institutional leaders may address some of the most compelling social issues facing our nation. This chapter is essentially about community colleges living up to and taking pride in their mission to be the "community's colleges." This involves two primary tasks: build community within the campus and build relationships with the community in which the campus is located. Both require creating a climate where students, faculty/staff, and community members feel cared for and welcomed. To be certain, community must be defined by the climate that is created (AACC, 2018). In other words, it is up to those who lead, work, and teach in community colleges to create a positive climate for those on and off campus. This will require a great deal of personal reflection and professional training. Merely providing myriad resources and support services to students will be ineffective unless faculty, staff, and administrators are not just accessible but also approachable and outgoing.

Rendón (2002) places the responsibility for outreach on the practitioner rather than the student. She argues many community college students are reluctant to approach faculty or staff because of past negative educational experiences. Some may be unsure of how to navigate the system of higher education. Simply put, "They cannot ask what they do not know" (p. 644). This is particularly the case when considering students in early college/dual enrollment programs, seniors interested in lifelong learning, and students facing food and housing insecurities. Thus, faculty and staff must take the initiative to get to know the students, their family backgrounds, and their personal and professional goals. At the same time, they must first see students as capable as opposed to deficient learners. They must build students' confidence and validate them in- and outside the classroom in a holistic way.

Bob's story about the math lab at GCC is important because Bob's response showed how campuses should respond to students on campus. Allowing students to "hang out" in a math lab tells them they belong, that this is their institution too. The story is particularly salient in light of ongoing racial profiling cases on college campuses that have made headlines across the country and made students question their relationship to the institution. For instance, in 2015 a Black male student at Kennesaw State University in Georgia was waiting to meet with his advisor. The advisor was delayed, the student sat down, and was accused of harassing the advisor. His charge: waiting while Black. In 2018 a Black graduate student was resting in the lounge during finals week at Yale University when another student called the police and accused her of napping while Black. Also, in 2018, two teenage brothers of the Mohawk Nation were detained and accused of "looking suspicious" when a white woman dialed 9-1-1 to report them while they were on a campus tour at Colorado State University. They were accused of "not belonging." While these particular incidents occurred on four-year college campuses, it shows what could have happened at GCC if Bob reacted differently to the security guard who phoned about students in the lab at night. Certainly, community colleges are not immune to racial profiling. As Bob's stories shed light on the multiple ways community colleges create community, it is equally important to shed light on issues the community college must still contend with as we look to them as the community's colleges. Indeed, if they are to continue to be the democratizing arm of higher education, they must be welcoming to all communities.

Racial profiling in community colleges may look different than in four-year institutions in part because it often takes place in classrooms, rather than larger community spaces. Some faculty may perceive students of color as less engaged or unmotivated simply by their appearance or who they sit with in class (Catallozzi, 2019). Black students in community colleges are more likely than their four-year peers to require developmental education, even after accounting for academic preparation (Attewell et al., 2006). Black community college students in developmental math often feel discriminated against and negatively stereotyped (Roberts, 2020). In Orellana (2019) students of color felt supported by faculty but also felt unvalued by faculty and white peers because diversity and racial issues were either not addressed or the faculty were uncomfortable or unprepared to discuss the subject matter. Some students expressed they sensed a "fear of diversity" among faculty and peers.

These experiences are not limited to the classroom and are not limited to students. Some faculty of color at community colleges experience the same types of racial microaggressions, stereotypes, and invalidation as students of color. For instance, Escalera-Kelley (2020) found Latinx community college faculty were criticized for speaking Spanish or "speaking with an accent" and were discredited and ignored by their white colleagues, particularly when advocating for Latinx students. One Latinx faculty member reflected, "I think part of it is the fear, fear of us and what we are saying" (p. 144). Interestingly, Escalera-Kelley's study took place at Hispanic-Serving community colleges, suggesting that community colleges need to reflect on the meaning of that federal designation and the fiscal support that comes along with it. These examples demonstrate that racism is alive and well at community colleges, and it threatens their mission.

The need for community college faculty, staff, and administrators to address these issues is critical to realizing a diverse democratic society. As Burke (2013) explained:

> Community colleges . . . play an important role in shaping the cultural norms within a community as one of the leading educational voices within each community. . . . Diversity planning in community colleges can create culturally inclusive environments to support and nurture the development of campus and local communities. (pp. 840–841)

To be a leader or a partner in the community, community colleges must maintain a climate that is welcoming of all. All members of the community must feel that they belong.

Community, then, may begin in the classroom, but it must extend throughout the entire college and into the community at large. AACC's (1988) *Building Communities* explained, "What we seek is a climate in which the social and the intellectual relationships are strengthened, one in which the classroom is extended" (p. 30). Community colleges aren't community colleges just because of their name; indeed, some two-year institutions dropped the name as they now offer bachelor's degrees. Some two-year institutions never had it in their name. Yet, to be a community and to be a part of one, the college must develop and nurture relationships with students, their faculty, and the public. As the AACC report urged, community "in its broadest and best sense, encompasses a concern for the whole, for integrations and collaboration, for openness and integrity, for inclusiveness and self-renewal" (p. 7).

Community colleges, for instance, may address food insecurities on campus and in the community by providing food pantries for their campus community (because food insecurities are not limited to students). Supporting seniors and providing childcare on campus also fill an urgent social need.

Additionally, campuses that offer police training are beginning to look at the way they train new officers via police academies as well as training their own police or security forces. Each year thousands of police officers, firemen, and paramedics enroll and train at the nation's two-year institutions, as 80% of all first responders in the United States are trained by community colleges. Indeed, the ex-officer convicted of killing George Floyd and the three other officers charged with his death attended a community college in Minnesota. Moreover, one of the officers involved in the murder of Rayshard Brooks was once a community college police officer in Massachusetts. Reviewing police training curricula and practices may help to address systemic racism within the police force. Rydberg and Terrill (2010), for instance, found officers who had some college education were significantly less likely to use force during officer encounters. Again, it is about creating

> a climate in which the social and the intellectual relationships are strengthened, one in which the classroom is extended. Properly conceived, the community should renew itself on every occasion when there is an interaction between the student and the college. (AACC, 1988, p. 30)

Helping to build an educated workforce and supporting the local economy, as Bob pointed out, is an important role for community college presidents and leaders. The workforce development mission of two-year institutions, at times placed at odds against the transfer mission, includes job skill development courses that may be credit or noncredit courses. During the recession of 2008–2010, many displaced workers looked to the community college to develop new skills for new jobs when their old ones were eliminated (Jacobs & Worth, 2019). The Obama administration supported this need through the Trade Adjustment Assistance Community College and Career Training (TAACCCT) program. Though the program ended in 2018, funds were provided to support staff development, purchase technical equipment, and develop collaborations between colleges, states, and industry. Nearly 60 grants were made to 60% of all community colleges (Jacobs & Worth, 2019).

Today, as we face new challenges as a result of great job loss during the COVID-19 health crisis, the future of workforce development within community colleges remains uncertain. Some of the uncertainty is because we don't know the full impact of COVID-19 on our economy and how it will shift workforce needs and required skills. We do know, however, that enrollment is declining and many facing an economic downturn are not looking to community colleges as much as they did in the past. The success of workforce development as we move in the future will depend on the flexibility community colleges have always shown over the years. This flexibility is what led many of their region's employees or future employees to the community college in the first place.

Discussion Questions

1. As an institutional leader, what type of climate do you seek to create?
2. How do you convey to the campus and larger community (including high school students, adult learners, seniors, and those seeking a bachelor's degree) that they are welcome on campus?
3. In what ways do leaders and institutional practitioners validate and support students? What factors prohibit validation and support?
4. How do leaders develop authentic relationships with the community?
5. What social challenges (e.g., food insecurity, racial injustice, etc.) can/should community colleges address?
6. What partnerships in your local community are most important to develop? What steps should be taken to foster these relationships/partnerships?
7. What are current challenges to the workforce development mission of community colleges?

4

LEADERSHIP MATTERS

Leadership and learning are indispensable to each other.

—John F. Kennedy

On my very 1st day as the president of GCC, I was riding the elevator to my new office with a box of my "stuff" in tow. A senior member of the faculty was also on that elevator heading up to the third floor. "Welcome to GCC," he said. "Thanks," I said in return, each of us aware of the uniqueness of the moment. He then said, "I bet you have heard that this college is a real snake pit, and particularly hard on presidents." "Well," I said. "Actually, yes, I have heard just that." In fact, I had friends and colleagues write or call urging me not to take the position. They said that GCC faculty and staff were crazy and that going there would be a career ender. "It must be in the water out there," they wrote.

The professor then said something I will never forget: "All we have ever looked for in a leader is someone as committed to students, this college, and our community as we are." GCC at the time had just voted overwhelmingly *against* a faculty contract that would increase salary significantly but added a fifth course to their workload. They voted against that contract, the only college in the state to do so overwhelmingly, knowing that they deserved the salary increase, but they all also understood the negative impact of that fifth course for students. "Wow," I thought to myself. "This is the place for me."

Being a student- and community-centered college was core to all at GCC. Significant change might be required at other institutions for the same to be true. As is often stated, change is the only constant, and that is certainly the case in higher education. Making those changes during a time of unprecedented disruption and uncertainty requires strong, innovative, and engaged leadership. The desired changes will not occur by presidents mandating it or making speeches toward that end. Faculty and college staff must be integral partners in the design and implementation of the desired change.

A growing gulf exists in the nation's colleges between the culture of administrative leadership and the teaching and learning culture of faculty and staff. The paradigms by which they are operating have become increasingly different and, in some cases, strained. All too often college leaders are trained in skill sets that might work well in nonacademic organizations, while faculty and staff are often committed to a very different set of values and assumptions. The language can be different, and at times even the goals are different. A clash of cultures is inevitable.

I find it ironic that academics such as Peter Senge, Karen Watkins, and Victoria Marsick are educating leaders of Fortune 500 companies about how to create "learning organizations," while many administrators in education are still being taught leadership from a corporate perspective. Sustaining change can only occur in a culture that supports the learning of all in the college community. There are many similarities between the role of college leadership and the role of a teacher in the learning process. Learning is about change. Change is dependent on learning. Good teachers understand that dynamic. They create environments for learning, develop skills that enable students to become empowered learners, establish clear goals, create safe environments for risk taking, and provide the necessary tools for success.

Teachers challenge, remediate, motivate, support, and reward. Why then should the role of college leadership be all that different? Successful college leaders understand how to facilitate and manage change in part by creating environments for people to learn. College faculty and staff come to the academy, after all, to become members of a community of learners. I encourage graduate schools and new leaders in higher education to engage in a dialogue about an evolving leadership model for college leaders that speaks to the culture of institutions designed for learning.

No one model of leadership fits all leaders, and no one model of leadership fits the need of all colleges. That said, according to the "AACC Competencies for Community College Leaders," there are a core set of competencies for aspiring CEOs that one can work toward: The authors identify 11. They state that an effective college leader

- embraces the mission, vision, and values of the community college acknowledging the college's past, and at the same time, building its future;
- is knowledgeable about governance and policies;
- supports student success across the institution, in all facets of the colleges;
- understands the importance of interpersonal relationships in the work to create a student-centered institution;

- is competent in all aspects of managing the college such as strategic planning, finances, facilities, accreditation, and technology;
- uses data to inform the decisions of the college;
- is a champion of community college ideals, and can engage key stakeholders to take action on behalf of the college;
- builds relationships to advance the community college agenda;
- demonstrates strong communication skills on campus and in the community;
- develops and maintains internal and external relationships that nurture diversity, and that promote the success of the college and the community it serves; and
- possesses and elevates those abilities that promote the community college agenda. (AACC, 2018, pp. 51–61)

On Mission

Philosopher Friedrich Nietzsche was right, being clear about the "why" provides clarity about the "how." That is why the New England Commission on Higher Education (NECHE) identifies "Mission" as "Standard One" for accreditation. The mission of any organization is the foundation on which all else is built. That is especially true in higher education. I think it is essential to establish the commitment to serve the community in a college's mission statement.

Mission statements are an incredibly important navigational tool for any college. By identifying the purpose of the college, you can better establish the goals. Once goals are set, the college can then develop a strategy. The mission statement is the foundation on which all is built and should be used to guide decisions on a regular basis. Budget, planning, curriculum, pedagogy, policy, and hiring decisions must be guided by the mission, or that misalignment will lead the college astray. Mission statements can influence how faculty and staff feel about their work and can help recruit new folks whose values are aligned with the college. The statement should communicate the college's passion and vision to all internally and in the community.

During the time I was the academic dean at Berkshire Community College, I taught two courses in the master of business administration (MBA) program of Western New England College. (It is now Western New England University.) Springfield was about 45 minutes away, and so the program was offered on our Pittsfield campus for Berkshire County residents. The two courses I taught were Organizational Behavior and the MBA program's capstone course.

One of the exercises/assignments I had for students in the capstone course was to develop mission statements. My students came from local businesses, industry, and the community hospital. I placed students in groups and assigned each the fictitious name of a business, hospital, and professional baseball team. Their task was to develop a mission statement.

In each of the three times I taught that course, the outcomes were similar. The baseball team and the two private corporations had no problem developing a mission statement. They were clear about purpose, outcomes, values, and means. That was not the case for those assigned to the hospital. Each group in each class assigned to the "Fair Care Health System" became conflicted about the primary focus and core mission. Some wanted the mission to primarily and explicitly focus on patients, while others in the group wanted to emphasize finance first. A lack of clarity about mission and purpose will create a lack of clarity about means to the end.

When Dewey spoke of the school as the social center, when Addams was leading Hull House, when Harper and Brown created Joliet Junior, and when the Truman Commission on Higher Education called for increased access to a college education in communities, they were all clear about mission. Each wrote with great passion and clarity about "why." Leaders understand the importance of mission and then work to create the environment, strategic plans, budgets, and assessment systems accordingly. Leaders work to create culture that embraces mission. In this time of acute disruption, all too many institutions lose their way for short-term gains, often too far adrift from the core mission of the institution. The short-term quarterly transactional path can lead an institution on a hazardous journey.

On Culture

I have always been pulled toward Margaret Wheatly's thinking and writing about organizational culture. I learned from her that organizations, like organisms, are living systems. It is an image and definition that fit well at GCC. I saw the college less as a machine with parts and numbers, as an engineer might, and more as a system of living and breathing people with feelings and intelligence, capable of learning and change.

I still have to chuckle when I hear leaders complain that people in their organizations are always resistant to change, especially so when presidents or provosts talk about faculty in higher education. That usually suggests to me that leaders either don't know how to create change or that the leader doesn't appreciate the possibility that faculty could be right about the opposition to change.

Leadership is vital to the creation and communication of a college's culture. However, the relationship between leadership and culture is two-way, not one-sided. While leaders are the principal architects of culture, an established culture also influences what kind of leadership is possible (Schein, 1985). Some refer to that as "fit."

Former Massachusetts Institute of Technology (MIT) Sloan School Professor Edgar Schein wrote that leadership is intertwined with culture formation, evolution, and transformation. He believed that cultural formation begins with the leader. Leaders are responsible for embedding culture by communicating what they care about. I have seen examples of leadership that are more transactional than transformational and less focused on values and core beliefs. It is up to the leadership of the college to create, strengthen, and reinforce the core culture.

When then President Byron McClenney delivered a speech to the faculty and staff of the Community College of Denver entitled "The Many Colors of Denver," he received a standing ovation. In addition to touching the hearts and minds of all in attendance, he was reinforcing and embedding values and beliefs about the importance of inclusion, diversity, equity, and social justice within the college culture.

Changing the culture of a college is hard work. Compliance can create change, but change that is top-down tends to be short-lived and not sustaining. Cultural change is a long-term project, requiring a longer term investment on the part of the leader and one that empowers all in the organization to engage in, plan for, and own the direction of cultural change. You just have to put in the time and the work.

The cultural change process can create a community of teachers and learners all rowing in the same direction toward meeting the mandates of the institutional mission, "by us, for us." The phrase, "by us, for us," was taken from the GCC 2010 NECHE accreditation self-study. I think of it as a wonderful statement of empowerment and ownership of the process by the faculty and staff involved. It is also a phrase that speaks to the commitment of betterment as the purpose of the work and not one of compliance.

GCC transferred more women to Smith College than any other community college in the nation. The Jack Kent Cook Foundation funded a study at the University of Southern California (USC) and the UMass Boston to assess the programs at community colleges with high transfer rates to private elite colleges. Given our transfer rate from GCC to Smith, the USC researchers came to visit with our students, faculty, and staff. The authors of that study decided *not* to include GCC in their final report because they could not identify a program that was replicable. Rather, along with the individual faculty that fostered the Smith pathway, it was the transfer emphasizing culture of the college that was found significant.

On Creating the Environment for a Community of Teachers and Learners

In a telephone conversation in 1998, Peter Senge told me the story of a principal he met in Oregon who said, "My primary job as principal is to create a learning environment for our teachers." If faculty and staff are held responsible for creating learning environments that facilitate, encourage, and foster learning for students, then college leadership must also be responsible for developing similar learning environments for faculty and staff. College faculty, staff, and leadership understand that change is the only constant, and that learning is about change. College leaders set the tone and create the environment in which learning and change can occur. While there are many, the one skill most transferable from the classroom to the president's conference room is the necessity to develop environments that support and encourage change.

In *The Courage to Teach*, Parker Palmer (1998) discusses the learning environment as "paradoxical tensions that [he] want[s] to build into the teaching and learning spaces" (p. 74). Each speak to an environment that facilitates learning and embraces change. He goes on to identify six:

1. *The space should be bounded and open.*
   According to Palmer (1998),

   > The boundaries around a teaching and learning space are created by using a question, a text, or a body of data that keeps us focused on the subject at hand. Within those boundaries, students are free to speak, but their speaking is always guided toward the topic. Space without boundaries is not space; it is a chaotic void, and in such a place no learning is likely to occur. But for a space to be a space it must be open as well as bounded—open to the many paths down which discussing may take us, to the surprise that always comes with real learning. If boundaries remind us that our joining has a destination, openness reminds us that there are many ways to reach that end. (pp. 74–75)

   I believe that there are many ways of getting from point A to point B as long as you know what point B looks like. The importance of having a vision of where you want to go cannot be overstated. So too is the process of discovery. Each college must find its own way. J. Krishnamurti

(1964) writes, "Discovery, not imitation, is the true essence of education" (p. 71). College leaders must possess the same courage all good teachers demonstrate every day in the process of teaching and learning, respecting and empowering their students to reach the established destination. Leaders must also respect and empower faculty and staff in that journey. All too often the traditional model of management teaches something very different. Peter Senge (1990) writes:

> Unfortunately, far too many university executives conclude that this implies a kind of passive leadership, an almost caretaker mentality. On the contrary, the challenges of executive leadership in a learning environment are, if anything, more demanding than are our traditional image of executives as "captains of the ship." They require executives who are designers, not just speechmakers. Those who understand this can have lasting influence. (p. 8)

This is our destination; let us talk about the journey.

2. *The space should be hospitable and charged.*

Palmer (1998) writes that "open space is liberating but it also raises the fear of getting lost in the uncharted and the unknown" (p. 74).

There is a wonderful section of *Cape Cod* when Henry David Thoreau (1961) and his companion are walking over the sand dunes and come across a hut for wayward sailors. Those huts had earned a reputation for uncertainty, and so the approach caused trepidation. Upon his arrival Thoreau found a little hole in that pine hut into which he was able to peer. With understandable apprehension he looked in and said, "For the pupil will be enlarged by looking. There never was so dark a night that a patient and persistent eye will not prevail over it" (p. 88). Learning can be frightening. People become secure with what they know. Good teachers know the fear of their students and understand how to chart a course and then help each student navigate the waters. They know when to step in to assist, and they also know when it is appropriate to take a step back and allow the student to experience the moment on their own. Good teachers also understand that students will not learn if the environment is too safe. Risk is necessary for students to achieve. Risk is inevitable in learning and essential for our faculty, staff, and colleges to grow. Why would we think that faculty and staff experience any less fear—need any less support, structure, direction, or encouragement to navigate their own journeys? How many colleges have asked faculty and staff to move forward in a new direction without any understanding of their learning curve? The college environment needs to be safe and charged for sustainable change.

3. *The space should invite the voice of the individual and the voice of the group.*

> If a space is to support learning, it must invite students to find their authentic voice. . . . Learning does not happen when students are unable to express ideas, emotions, confusion, ignorance, and prejudice. Only when people can speak their minds does education have a chance to happen . . . but, the space must also amplify the voice of the group—affirming, questioning, and challenging the voice of the individual. (Palmer, 1998, pp. 75–76)

I have observed that good teachers know that with the individualized balance of structure and support, students open up and ask that "dumb" question or dare to challenge the prevalent idea—"a real goose bump moment," as one of my colleagues once said. Real-deal teachers help students develop their voice and the courage to express it. College leaders must be as attentive to this paradox as classroom teachers. Those who help build policies will support them. Getting faculty engaged in the change process is as critical as the desired outcome. It is too easy for college faculty and staff to grow silent and disengage. It is too damaging to the college to allow that to happen. College leaders need to encourage the voice of individual faculty, staff, and students as well as respect the voice of the collective. Balancing the individual voice alongside the collective voice of a community is not the work for the weak of heart.

4. *The space should honor the "little" stories of the individual and the big stories of the disciplines and traditions.*

Like our faculty do for students, college leaders must develop environments that listen to the individual stories of faculty and the big stories of our disciplines and our mission.

Projected retirements have come to fruition. The good news is that this moment provides the opportunity to recruit and select new faculty and staff passionate about students, brimming with new ideas and robust energy, and their learning. The downside is the loss of talented and experienced faculty and staff who carry with them the history of our colleges. Whether through formal mentor programs or through informal conversations in the hallways, it is most beneficial for those new faculty to have the opportunity to listen and learn from those who are retiring. How rich their experiences have been and how important their stories are. Orientation programs for new faculty and staff provide the opportunity to inculcate new members into the college culture. Professional development programs, created to provide faculty and staff the opportunity to tell the stories of teaching and learning, accomplish that goal as well. It is within those relationships, orientations, and development programs that the little stories of the faculty and staff of the college, as well as the big stories of the disciplines and traditions, can be told.

5. *The space should support solitude and surround it with resources of community.* Learning demands both solitude and community. There is a profound need for community on our nation's campuses. Students and faculty alike report a heightened sense of stress and isolation. While the causes are considerable and complex, impacted by economic, social, and technological conditions, the challenge to create community is as formidable to college leaders as it is to faculty. At the same time, I think that the need to get out on the balcony for reflection is significant. The time for solitude and reflection provides the time for critical analysis and integration. Time then, in a world sped up and downsized, is one of higher education's richest resources. Good teachers understand how to create climates of interconnectivity and engagement. It is all too easy for anomic slippage to occur. Students do not learn in isolation; neither do faculty. People also need time and space alone to learn. College leadership should support the solitude of individual members of the faculty but also understand the paradoxical need to belong to a community of learners.

6. *The space should welcome both silence and speech.*
Some of the longest moments in a class are the silent ones. Yet good teachers understand just how important that silence is. The instinct is to fill the void. The courage to allow students to hear themselves, to reflect, or to amass the courage to speak is paramount among the strongest members of our faculty. It is not a moment for the skittish—not for students, not for teachers. Effective teachers also know that if the silence is left to fester too long, it can lay atop the excitement of discovery like the effect of a heavy morning fog along the Maine coast for sailors eager to set sail. The magic is in the moment. How long one waits is the expertise that teachers bring to the moment. It is their intuitive timer that goes off, after reading body language and their students' eyes, suggesting that it is time to intervene. It is a skill that is developed over many years of teaching, learning, and engagement. College leaders would do well to develop that same level of balance and understanding.

On Accreditation

As the CAO, it was important to me to wait until the New England Association of Schools and Colleges (NEASC) visiting team's exit review at Berkshire Community College before I headed out to GCC in 2000. The president at BCC had asked me to oversee the writing of the self-study.

Led by two faculty members with great integrity who were highly respected by all at the college, the process and end result at Berkshire was worth the time and sweat equity. Those two faculty chairs were wonderful to work with and provided great service to the college.

The 90-minute drive from Pittsfield to Greenfield over the picturesque Berkshire Hills is as beautiful in December as it is in July. I arrived at GCC soon after the college had also gone through its self-study. A NEASC team had just concluded their visit to GCC as well. It was a perfect transitional moment for a new president. I learned a great deal about GCC's sense of its strengths, concerns, and projections into the future from that 2000 self-study. I couldn't have asked for a better introduction, alongside the visiting team's observations and perspectives.

I have been involved in five self-studies, the last two as president at GCC. I was a member of one visiting team, chaired three visiting teams, and served as a commissioner of the NECHE. I learned a great deal over the course of those years and can honestly say that my NECHE experiences were the best professional development of my career.

There is a dual purpose of accreditation: to foster improvement and to assure quality. I have seen and experienced firsthand the New England accreditation process achieve those ends in brilliant fashion. New England has some of the most prestigious institutions of higher education whose accreditation was in little doubt. Yet at each turn of the cycle, even the elite of the elite made the most of the opportunities, empowering and developing their faculty and staff in the process.

I was most pleased and proud of all involved at GCC when the cochairs of our self-study team for 2010 were asked to present their work at a NECHE conference. That GCC leadership team did an outstanding job in both process and product. As president, I chose the leaders, approved the standards teams, and then empowered them to do the work. The team was respectful to all at the college, ensuring constant two-way communication. I trusted them and trusted the process. They trusted me in return. It served our college well, building community and elevating our work toward excellence.

That 2010 self-study was an important document as well as a process for GCC. The means to achieve that end were the ends in the making. Our work was not one of compliance simply looking for a check in the approval box. Rather, our college understood the opportunity to do the work "by us, for us," which was the working mantra of the self-study team. If there is a better way to develop faculty buy-in for planning and shared governance, I am not aware of it. We used the NECHE accreditation process for improvement, accountability, professional development, empowerment, ownership, and shared governance. It is one thing to get a self-study done solely for the purpose of accreditation, and I do not understate the importance of that. However, it is yet another level of commitment to dive in fully and appreciate the opportunity for betterment. If I had to do my presidency all over again, I would have more fully integrated the commission's standards and the accreditation cycle into the shared governance and planning structures of the college.

The U.S. Secretary of Education and the Council for Higher Education Accreditation (CHEA) accredits the accreditors of the United States. Seven regional accreditors have the responsibility for 7,000 institutions and 18,000 programs. NECHE has responsibility for 229 colleges and universities. There are 27 commissioners, 10.5 staff members (five professionals; 5.5 support), and hundreds of volunteers. Each are amazing educators—truly. I have so much respect for each and every commissioner I served with.

The relationship between institutional members and the commission is ongoing. Each college or university engages in a full self-study for re-accreditation at least once every 10 years. They are required to submit an interim report at the midpoint of the cycle, an annual report, and special reports and/or focused visits as recommended by commission. At NECHE, accreditation = standards + mission. That is to say, there was respect and understanding of the mission vis-à-vis standards. The standards of NECHE are as follows:

1. Mission and Purposes
2. Planning and Evaluation
3. Organization and Governance
4. The Academic Program
5. Students
6. Teaching, Learning, and Scholarship
7. Institutional Resources
8. Educational Effectiveness
9. Integrity, Transparency, and Public Disclosure (NECHE, 2021)

The NECHE 10-year cycle of accreditation is an elegant tool for assessment and improvement. As a commissioner I learned the difference between standards and standardization, and I learned about the power of the aspirational process rather than one of compliance. Sign me up for standards and the aspirational journey. New England commissioners were sensitive to individual missions, context, and the nuances of its member colleges and universities. The commission pushed, pulled, and cajoled each institution toward improvement while living up to its responsibilities to the public and key stakeholders, and students and their families. That balance and philosophical framework was led by leader and teacher Barbara Brittingham. I have always been most appreciative of NECHE as a college president, a commissioner, a visiting team leader, and especially so as a parent of a student at an accredited institution.

From Beethoven to Betterment

I was the CAO at Berkshire Community College for about 5 and a half years. One of the things our family loved to do in the summer while living in Pittsfield was to attend rehearsals of the Boston Symphony Orchestra (BSO) at Tanglewood. The venue was magic. We brought our blankets, chairs, coffee, and bagels. I remember attending a rehearsal for Beethoven's Symphony No. 9, which is always the culmination of the Tanglewood season. We found our spot on the lawn, set down our things, and sat back. The conductor of the BSO at the time was Seigi Ozawa. On the blanket next to us was a retired public school music teacher from Ohio and his family. As we talked I learned that attending Tanglewood was on his bucket list. Check.

The BSO began to play, gaining the attention of all in attendance. It did not take long before the music began to intensify, a purposeful slow and steady crescendo. We were soon standing, now on the edge of the lawn at the back of the Koussevitzky shed. The sounds of "Ode to Joy" began to fill the grounds of Tanglewood as much as it did our hearts. My daughter, then 4 years old, was on my shoulders, the retired band teacher from Ohio to my left. I looked over and watched the tears roll down his cheeks. The music built in its intensity, coming to a thunderous end. All in the shed and all on the lawn immediately stood and cheered in exaltation. "Bravo!" we shouted. "Bravo! Bravo!"

As the cheers faded into silence, there really wasn't much to be said. No words could communicate all that we were thinking, feeling, and experiencing, so we gathered our belongings and started out to our cars. But just then, and to my great surprise, I heard the BSO playing the last few bars of the symphony one more time! Here were some of the finest musicians in the world having so beautifully completed a musical piece, affirmed by the shouts of the audience, and the conductor says, "Let's play those last few sections one more time." By doing so, Seigi Ozawa was saying to those musicians, "We can do better."

I remember sharing that story with the faculty and staff at GCC. It resonated with all in the room. They understood that excellence was a journey more than it was a destination and that students deserved our very best.

Atul Gawande (2007), writer, teacher, and surgeon, communicated that point best when he wrote:

> Betterment is a perpetual labor. The world is chaotic, disorganized, and vexing, and medicine (education) is nowhere spared that reality. To complicate matters, we in medicine (education) are also only humans ourselves. We are distractible, weak, and given to our own concerns. Yet still, to live as

a doctor (educator) is to live so that one's life is bound up in others' and in science (teaching and learning) and in the messy, complicated connection between the two. It is to live a life of responsibility. The question, then, is not whether one accepts the responsibility. Just by doing this work, one has. The question is, having accepted the responsibility, how one does such work well? (p. 11)

More than a strategic tool, the process of betterment is a philosophical framework for the long-term journey toward excellence. One never arrives. Means are the ends in the making. How a college works day in and day out to achieve its goals and meet the mandates of its mission defines that college. Each layer of the college is connected and interrelated. Excellence begets excellence, and betterment is a daily practice.

On Facilities Planning

Asbestos was found in the buildings of GCC in the mid-1990s, and the first phase of the abatement project started a few years before I arrived in 2000. Because of the hard work and support of local legislators, trustees, and community leaders, over $100 million of state and federal funds were ultimately invested in the college's buildings by the time all the capital projects were completed in 2010. The impact was far greater than I had ever imagined.

The Commonwealth of Massachusetts, not the college, is responsible for all abatement and refurbishment costs. The first phase of that project started in 1998, and it did not go well. Delays and charges of poor work on the part of the contractors led to litigation. I began my tenure at GCC just as "Phase 1: The North" was coming to a conclusion. It was imperative that the second phase not replicate the mistakes of the first, so I asked as many college staff and state officials as I could about what had happened and what we learned. It was clear to me that a very short-term perspective and short-term strategy on the part of the contractors created many of the problems. It was now our turn. Next up, "Phase 2: The South."

As the second phase unfolded, we wanted to be sure that we were looking far enough down the road with our plans while at the same time repairing the present. We had the opportunity to think outside the box; we had support in Boston and a good, smart team on campus. The second phase was completed without problem, adding significantly to the teaching and learning environment on campus. Looking back, I realize now that the second phase was just practice; the real challenge was about to begin.

The Core project started in 2007. The "Core" was the center of the campus, hence the "North" and "South" in the phases. The library; food services; admissions, registrar, advising, testing/assessment, and administrative offices; bookstore; TV studio; lecture hall; and student life were all housed in the Core. We worked with the Department of Capital Assets and Management (DCAM) to plan for its closing and the asbestos abatement. This was no small challenge. Where the heck where we going to place those services, programs, and offices? But we did. We rented a storage facility for many of our library books, reestablished a small food services area, and moved people to places around the campus that were makeshift, to say the least. I must say that with all that disruption, the college community handled it quite well. Good communication on our part mattered. But most of all there was an understanding on campus that the building was going to become a healthier place to teach, learn, and work. Space matters, buildings matter, and teaching and learning matter. Space designed specifically to teach, learn, and work matters. And people matter most, so the campus community understood and embraced the moment; they trusted us.

The Core was closed, and the abatement began. Our journey was underway. One of the worst decisions I made during that time had to do with the walls of "the tunnel." We built a wooden tunnel to allow people to move between the south and north buildings under some cover. After a couple of requests and discussions with student leaders and their faculty advocates, I approved a policy that would allow people to write and draw on the wooden, temporary walls of that tunnel during construction. This was not a good idea! The truth is that 99.9% of the drawings and writing on the wall were respectful, at times insightful, and in a few cases quite humorous. But there were the few. There were a couple of comments that were disrespectful and a few drawings that were inappropriate for public space. Ultimately, we painted over the inner walls of that tunnel. We dealt with it, learned from it, and moved forward as a college community. Who the heck made that decision? Oh, right; it was me.

The Core was laid bare, and the inside walls taken down by the time the "Great Recession" hit the economic fan. "What do you mean there is no money for the completion of the project?" The governor at that time, Deval Patrick, made the short flight down to DC to meet with President Obama to help develop the American Recovery and Reinvestment Act (ARRA) of 2009. Of the $787 billion ARRA funds approved and allocated for the nation, Patrick came back with $14 billion for the commonwealth. We knew we were going to have to fight to get our fair share.

Within a short period of time, it was announced that GCC was going to be one of the five colleges to receive ARRA funds for capital projects. "Whew!

Okay, we can go forward." As soon as I received the email announcing we were going to work with Gensler, who won the capital project bid, I searched the Web to learn as much as I could about the firm. Their website said that Gensler was "a global architecture, design, planning and consulting firm with 49 locations across Asia, Europe, Australia, the Middle East and the Americas" (Gensler, n.d., para. 1). I thought, "Wowzah, could this be the same group?" It was. Gensler is a worldwide firm and had many significant buildings in their portfolio. Ken Fisher was going to be the lead architect. Within a couple of days he wrote to me and wanted to set up a meeting to talk about the project.

I called him immediately and got to the point quickly: "Ken, you are a big company with a large portfolio. We are the smallest college in the poorest county in Massachusetts." I then added with as much clarity and the same tone as my mother did when she wanted to make it clear that I had better not mess up, "Ken, this might be just another project for you, but this is our once-in-the-college's-lifetime opportunity to create a first-class building for our students and this community. Do you understand?" He did, truly; he really did get it.

At that first meeting Ken and his wonderfully creative team wanted to hear less about the building and more about GCC's mission and values and our vision for the future. We talked about being student centered, invested in building community, and how we valued belonging and relationships. We said that our facility must be committed to environmental sustainability—and natural light. We love light; light is good for life, and light is good for learning. Balancing the desire for more glass, more light, and environmental sustainability was challenging. We did not want to have a large gap between what we were teaching in our Alternative and Sustainable Energy Associate Degree program and what we put into practice on our campus. But we wanted more light. The Green Campus Committee was helpful toward that end. Together, our college team and the Gensler design team planned for spaces and a building that reflected the core values of our college. We developed three different plans not knowing exactly how much would be allocated: an $18 million, $24 million, and a $31.5 million project. The $18 million plan was okay, the $24 million was good, but $31.5 million was transformational—a real step into the future and a powerful statement to the students, faculty, staff, and community. We understood the moment; it was on us now to get it done—and it was imperative that we get it done right.

Things were going along as well as I would have hoped when one day our administrative vice president (VP) asked me out of a meeting. He was ashen faced. He had just received a "heads-up" from a friend of his in Boston who told him, "Tell the president that he needs to cool it with the

$31.5 million request. He is going to get $18 million—and he is going to have to be happy with that or it will go down to $12 million." The VP then added a sentence I will never forget: "Tell your boss he doesn't want to be the butterfly that started the tsunami." He doesn't want to be the butterfly that starts the tsunami? Who says that? I had been in state service since 1978, so I had seen a lot and heard a lot with regard to the rough and tumble of state politics. We were not going to back down. We had a responsibility to this college and to this community; we just couldn't let them down. "Okay," I thought, "game on!"

I won't go into detail on the discussions of that time, but let me just say that the ultimate funding of the $31.5 million Core Capital Project at GCC was a reflection of a strong commitment from the local state delegation, DCAM leadership, and a few friends of the college—in all the right places, at exactly the right time. It is also important to note that the Core project came along at an economic moment that was not good for the nation but most beneficial to GCC. Steel prices were down, and construction companies needed the work. The college got our money's worth—and then some. Not only did we get that $31.5 million, but that money went further than we had ever hoped for.

The day we cut the ribbon on the new Core building felt a little surreal. Together we built a building that was LEED Gold certified; had a new barrier-free main entrance that replaced a 44-step entry; had improved overall connection and circulation between all wings of the college with the addition of connector corridors; had new windows, insulation, and roofing; and had implemented an integrated building system for the maintenance of the building. The new library was the jewel of the campus it was always meant to be. We transformed a dark and mobility-challenged building into a light, bright, and award-winning design for sustainability and accessibility. Our college team, Gensler's team, the DCAM team, and Barr and Barr contracting team built a first-class building for teaching, learning, and community for the smallest and poorest county in the state, a true "balancing wheel of the social machine."

There are many memories of that project that I will carry with me always, and among them was the time I overheard two students talking in the library, just after the building had opened. One said to the other, "I can't believe this is our college. . . . This is better than some of the buildings at the Five Colleges." Another was when one of our deans told me within months after the opening that "walking around GCC and seeing everyone smiling all the time was like when [they were] working at Syracuse University when [they] had just made it to the finals of March Madness." And when the chamber breakfast was held in our new dining common for the first time the community gave a standing ovation in appreciation for the project.

I remember saying at the ribbon cutting ceremony, "We finally have the buildings that match the excellence of our faculty and staff." That was the truth. From 2000–2010, we renovated the entire college campus, a facility built in 1973, for $100 million. But in the final analysis, all those capital projects, as beautiful and wonderful as they were, are simply a reflection of what the faculty and staff brought to GCC every day. We left it better than the way we found it. I loved all of that; I loved the final project, and I have to say I loved the process. We did good.

On Development

I don't know of a college that worked any harder in service to its community than GCC, and I don't know of a community that supported its college more than our community supported GCC. The Foundation was a most significant bridge in that relationship, more so than simply a vehicle for fundraising. Annual campaigns in the poorest county in any state would be most challenging, to say the least. Yet GCC raised more funds per Full Time Equivalency (FTE) than any other community college in the commonwealth and more total dollars than most.

Part of the reason for that support is found in the origins of the college and its Foundation. Both were borne of and by the community. Those roots are strong, and they manifest in many ways, including resources for the college. Leadership at the college, the trustees, the Foundation board, and the Foundation staff changed over the years, but the relationship between the college and community is baked into the culture and DNA of both.

That said, leadership does matter, and the impact of strong leadership is yet another reason for the foundation's success. The GCC Foundation Board has been a source of passion, wisdom, and guidance. The leadership and hard work of the foundation staff were equally impactful, especially with the executive directors. Strategic planning and event and investment planning alongside the work of volunteer coordination and training kept everyone pretty darn busy. Ask anyone in development and they will tell you that at the heart of raising money is the mission and the authenticity of friend-raising. It is the building and maintenance of relationships that matter most, and that was the job of all involved.

Asking for money is challenging and uncomfortable for many people. I found it easy because I was asking for the college and our students. A member of the faculty once told a group of volunteers at a campaign kickoff, "I know it is hard for some of you to ask for money, but please keep in mind that you are actually giving people an opportunity to feel good about doing good, and people want that in their lives." This is a nice perspective.

A significant shift in a college president's time with regard to resource development has occurred over the past 40 years. Fundraising is a pretty new area of work for community college leaders. There are reasons for that. I started working for the community colleges of Massachusetts in 1978. About 98% of a college budget at that time was state funded. About 48% of the fiscal year (FY) 2018 budget at GCC was state funds. The cost to students for an education increased significantly during those 40 years as a result.

It was also abundantly clear that a fundamental shift in funding for public higher education had occurred. Each college now needed to raise its own funds for new initiatives, scholarships, and equipment. A president at another community college in Western Massachusetts would say, "We used to be state funded, then we were state assisted, and now we are state located." The decline in state funding for higher education was not unique to the commonwealth. The reduction in state funding that began in 1980 shifted the cost of education to students and the attention of every community college president toward development. I would estimate that the shift in time allocation reflected the shift in funding, about 50%. The demand, however, for engagement and leadership internally did not diminish. That balance is determined not by a preplanned formula but more so by the ability of the president to have the pulse of the organization.

Not many community colleges even had fundraising capacity in 1980. Today every community college depends on those resources, and each president allocates the needed time to achieve those ends. Many point to the increase in student cost, student debt, and dependency on local fundraising as evidence of the privatization of public higher education. Hopefully the recent call for free community colleges will turn out as significant as the quantum shift that occurred in 1980.

The GCC Foundation became a very strong vehicle of community support. The annual campaign was the driver of that bus, and it has been a most successful journey. We raised just under $15 million from 2000–2018 for scholarships, college support, and the endowment. Alumni events, turkey trots, corn mazes, trivia nights, house parties, and the like were all wonderful friend-raisers, but it was the annual campaign that was the real-deal meat and potatoes of the Foundation's powerful impact.

Getting the college's first million-dollar gift for an endowed nursing faculty chair was a beautiful experience. Of course, the money mattered, but it was the heartfelt nature of the gift and its impact that I remember most. Mr. and Mrs. Anonymous were very special to the college and had been for many years. They had created a scholarship for all employees at their company who wanted to attend GCC. They continued their support for the college after they sold that business.

Their annual gift was significant enough that they made it a matching gift, wanting the college to use it to grow the campaign. It raised not only more money, but it raised the profile of the campaign in the community. I remember talking with those donors about the joys of a lobster roll as we sat outdoors eating our lunch near their summer home on the coast of Maine. The conversation shifted away from lobster and American history, Mr. Anonymous's favorite topic, to the possibility of an endowed faculty position in nursing. Although they had funded an early college program for at-risk high school students, it was the nursing program that was their most passionate point of giving. For example, they funded the ability of our nursing students to travel to points of the globe to learn and work in many different cultures, and they gave a significant part of their annual gift to the nursing program. So, bringing up the endowed faculty position seemed like a good fit.

Two or three conversations later, and with the extra support of our board chair, who was a friend of theirs, they agreed to the gift. Mr. and Mrs. Anonymous could have had a building with their name on it at Bowdoin College or another like it, but instead they chose GCC. They understood just how impactful their gift would be for students, college, and community. I am not sure if we were the first or second college in the state to get a million-dollar gift, but it felt transformative on many levels. Community college development had taken another step forward.

The dollars raised every year at GCC were a reflection of a strong relationship between college and community. Those who led, volunteered, made the calls, attended the events, asked for money, stuffed those packets, entered the data, and gave their hard-earned money, whether it was $1 or $1 million, they all got it. The community understood the importance of having GCC in the community, and the college took its mission and commitment to students and community to heart. It was a beautiful relationship. I can imagine Professor Dewey standing up at a Foundation event talking about colleges as the social center of a community. They would have loved him in Greenfield.

On Governance

The governance of community colleges across the 50 states is unique to each state, evolving from unique state circumstances. As a result of that unique state evolution, community colleges vary widely in the forms of local governance. And for those that are similar in structure, the impact of the head of that system defines that structure in ways that distinguish each system in each state. The Virginia community college system, for example, is as different from the Massachusetts system as Connecticut is from California. That is true not only by the structural design but by the impact of leadership as well. Some states are more centralized, with a chancellor or commissioner at the helm and decisions for each of the state colleges made in that office, while other states prefer a more decentralized system with the boards of trustees legally empowered to make decisions at the local level. Some states elect a board of trustees, while in others trustees are appointed by the governor. Some college boards empower college presidents with the decisions impacting the campus, while others require those decisions be made at the board level.

Throughout my 18 years as president, I was fortunate to work in a decentralized state system with a board of trustees made up of local leaders who cared deeply about the college, fortunate in that the governance model fit my style of leadership and our college culture. I don't believe that one size fits all in education. At GCC we made the most of the decentralized opportunity, form fitting education, as best we could, to individual student need. One of my favorite quotes from a member of the community is, "Getting an education at GCC was like buying a suit from a tailor and not one off the rack." Our student success data supported our approach.

The GCC Board of Trustees was appointed by the governor. They provided the guidance, ensured the accountability, and gave us the support that lifted our college and ensured that GCC was meeting the mandates of its mission. I was fortunate. On occasion, a board member weighed into places and in ways that were less than beneficial to all. But they were the outliers, not the norm. On those rare occasions, it was the chair who stepped into that space.

All the chairs of the GCC board, from my first reception to my last retirement party, were the absolute best: a community bank president, a retired university provost, a lawyer, an insurance company CEO, and a real estate mogul. Each was an alum, family of an alum, or hired an alum in their place of business. Each brought a very different skill set, political perspective, and leadership style to the table, but they all had five things in common: (a) They were all very smart, (b) they loved the college, (c) they loved the community, (d) they were all local community leaders, and (e) they all "got it." I learned from and benefited a great deal from each. There was a mutual respect and a mutual love for college and community. We always found the path to the same page no matter the issue so that the college would be on that page as well. Those board chairs understood their role and mine, their responsibilities and mine, and they understood leadership; they were just awesome. That relationship, between president and board chair, and/or between president and the CEO of the state system, sets a tone—be it functional or dysfunctional—that is felt in every classroom, office, and lab of a college. Every sitting president knows just how important those relationships are to the success of the college and its service to community.

Just as governance structures are unique to each state, the major changes in state-level community college governance over the past 50 years have taken place because of unique state circumstances. According to a paper developed for the state of Nevada by the National Center for Higher Education Management Systems (NCHEMS), the major governance changes, organized according to common themes, were as follows:

- *Consolidating two-year institutions under a single community and technical college board.* North Carolina (1979), Kentucky (1997), Louisiana (1998), and West Virginia (2000) established consolidated state community (and technical) college systems under statewide governing boards.
- *Expanding the mission of an existing technical college system.* Indiana (2005), Maine (2003), and New Hampshire (1999) transitioned technical college systems to comprehensive community colleges.
- *Consolidating of community and technical colleges and access-oriented state universities under a single governing board.* Minnesota (1995) and Connecticut (2011) consolidated community and technical college boards under a statewide board.
- *Consolidating oversight of locally governed community colleges under a statewide university governing board.* Kansas (1999) moved the statewide oversight of the locally governed community colleges from the State Board of Education to the Board of Regents, but the community colleges retained their local governing authority.
- *Eliminating a state-level coordinating board for locally governed community colleges.* Arizona (2003), a state with local elected boards and financing that includes local tax support, state appropriations, and tuition, abolished the state-level coordinating board for community colleges.
- *Strengthening a community college system to align with statewide goals for college completion.* Tennessee (2010) enacted the Complete College Tennessee Act, which strengthened the existing community colleges as a "system" within the governing authority of the Tennessee Board of Regents. (McGuinness, 2014)

On Hiring, Firing, Developing, and Sustaining College Leaders

I don't believe in cleaning house when you arrive at a college as a new president. Unless there were prior discussions with the board chair, I first assume that the existing cabinet-level leadership can do the work. I feel that this is also their college, home, and their community, so I believe in giving each the opportunity to succeed. I believe that it was up to me as a leader to get those folks on the same navigational page, all rowing in the same direction. If they didn't measure up, yes, I knew how to deal with that as well. I had the responsibility to make those tough decisions when the work wasn't getting done. Failure to make a change can be as detrimental as acting too soon. Both the inability to make the change and making change too soon can be most disruptive to the college community. Getting a true assessment of the college and the performance of the staff and faculty is essential to the work of your 1st year as president. Reading existing documents, building trusting relationships through candid and confidential conversations, and being clear about expectations from day 1 provides the snapshot and the roadmap for the long journey ahead.

I would always emphasize the importance and the opportunity of every vacancy to our search committees at GCC. "Never settle," I would say. After all, it is the faculty and staff of a college that make good on its promises. I changed the hiring process when I first arrived at the college and required committees to send three finalists to me for final selection. I invited the chair of the committee, the supervisor, and the VP to sit with me for the final decision. I wanted the college to emphasize the importance of every search.

I always found it frustrating and ironic that we in education were not good at providing learning opportunities for faculty and staff. We placed computers on office desks, smartboards in classrooms, leaders in key positions; embraced the commitment to developmental education; focused on assessment; saw an increase in mental health issues in our students; hired faculty to teach and staff to support students; and turned to remote learning all without the needed professional development. And because public education has been underfunded and in decline since 1980, professional development funds were usually among the first to be cut. I wanted to do something different on campus and statewide.

The Community College Leadership Academy (CCLA) and Teaching and Learning were statewide professional development programs in Massachusetts that I helped to develop. The former was created to develop future leaders for the community colleges of the commonwealth. The latter was created to bring faculty and staff together to discuss topics of concern that mattered most to those who teach.

Teaching and Learning came about when Jan Motta, then executive director of the Community Colleges of Massachusetts, and I talked about the fact that but for a few national conferences (AACC, National Institute for Staff and Organizational Development [NISOD], The League for Innovation) there were no professional development opportunities for our faculty and staff. We created a small working group, and, in the fall of 2000, the first Teaching and Learning conference was held at Mount Wachusett Community College in Gardener, Massachusetts. Each year since 2000, Teaching and Learning brought hundreds of faculty members and staff from around the state to teach and learn, together.

Endorsed by all 15 community college presidents, to create CCLA, Jan Motta and I met with Pat Crosson, then recently retired as faculty member, former provost at UMass Amherst, and newly appointed trustee at GCC. Soon after, we invited Joe Berger, then faculty member in the School of Education at UMass Amherst, to join the group. The mission of CCLA is to provide an avenue through which community colleges can prepare their future leaders while supporting existing talent. Starting in 2003, CCLA had a 15-year run developing 450 leaders of the community colleges of Massachusetts.

Kay McClenney, founding director of the Community College Survey of Student Engagement (CCSSE) and now senior advisor to the CEO and president of AACC, would often talk about the need for college presidents to stay at one place long enough to get something done. Most faculty and college staff know when someone has arrived on campus to build a resume or when someone is truly invested in college and community. Faculty and staff will, for the most part, wait out the former and work shoulder to shoulder with the latter. The national average for the tenure of college presidents continues to decline. In 2015 it was 6.5 years, and the post-pandemic predictions of departures have already begun. Whether it is the challenges of the job, greener pastures, or just one of the signs of the times, for community college presidents, the number is even lower today.

The hiring of a new president is absolutely the most important decision a board of trustees will make. It is a multimillion-dollar decision that impacts college and community alike. It truly is an investment in democracy at the local community level. Knowing what the college needs is step one, and that is not always as simple as it sounds. How well prepared are boards for that decision and that moment? Who is responsible for their readiness? It is alarming and unfortunate to have seen so many good boards with all good intentions miss the target. It is also exhilarating and joyful to see the selection of the right person at the right time. Hiring is job #1, job #2, and job #3!

If higher education is to step up to the plate and make good on the promises of our national experiment in democracy, leadership will matter.

Leadership will be required to elevate the relationship between college and community. The good news is that examples of that leadership can be found today throughout the nation.

Reflections

On Tuesday, February 5, 2008, then senator Barack Obama said, "Change will not come if we wait for some other person or some other time. We are the ones we've been waiting for. We are the change that we seek" (Obama, 2008, 18:52). This chapter calls on those of us in higher education in general, and in community colleges in particular, to be the leaders we seek. Instead of perpetuating the idea that college leaders must follow corporate leaders, Bob suggested college leaders should be more like educators and teachers. He states, "Teachers challenge, remediate, motivate, support, and reward," and he calls on college leaders to do the same. In other words, just like the institutions they serve, as community colleges aren't the community's colleges because of their name, presidents aren't leaders just because of the positions they hold. Leaders, like the best teachers, learn.

The issue of accreditation illustrates this point. Quality and accountability are concerns for higher education around the world (Blanco Ramirez, 2013). In the United States, all accrediting bodies generally focus on quality, student achievement, accountability for performance and transparency, standards, policies, and practices (CHEA, 2019). As Bob recognizes, assumptions are embedded within accrediting practices (Blanco Ramirez, 2013), so it is important for institutional leaders to know how their values and culture fulfill their mission. There is a difference between a college's commitment to standards, as opposed to standardization and the aspirational process rather than one of compliance.

Too many college administrators think accreditation reports are to show how their institution complies with policy and procedures. On the contrary, GCC "understood the opportunity to do the work 'by us, for us,' which was [their] working mantra" (p. 68, this volume). The goal for GCC wasn't to simply comply with accreditation mandates; it was to improve, hold themselves accountable, and create a sense of ownership at the institution.

When Daymond John and three of his friends started their clothing line, FUBU, in 1992, many big-name companies were targeting Black youth to buy their sportswear. None of these companies were Black owned. John, Keith Perrin, J. Alexander Martin, and Carl Brown decided to create their own clothing company that would be for Blacks, by Blacks, or "for us, by us" (FUBU). John and his friends recognized that by creating an emotional connection to their clothes, as FUBU did, they were able to increase their sales because people wanted to be a part of that. Indeed, Bob learned this lesson with his colleagues at GCC. By engaging in the accreditation self-study as an opportunity for betterment, rather than compliance, the college functioned at a higher level and demonstrated a higher level of commitment. Members of the self-study team recognized their role in shared governance by recognizing betterment at the institution was something they would create for others and for themselves.

Taking on this type of work is also a risk. Risk is an important part of leadership because it is what happens when one has a vision for something better. Rather than seeing a tunnel that merely kept people warm during colder months at GCC, Bob saw an opportunity to build community. Things may not have worked out the way he had planned or hoped, but he took the risk. He had the vision to create community, and he had the vision to recognize and learn from a mistake.

A part of this vision at GCC was the determination to ensure the campus buildings exemplified the excellence of the community. The Core project, for example, was not meant to "gentrify" the campus or compete with four-year colleges. As Warren (2017) so aptly pointed out, trying to directly compete with or emulate four-year institutions is an unnecessary battle that detracts from the community college mission. Building spaces that develop community and make those on campus feel good about being there, however, is a worthy endeavor and a model of success.

This chapter also highlights the way understanding organizational culture is key to success for leaders. By understanding the culture, Bob was able to create change with his campus community (by them, for them). This is an important point for any new community college leader. Building relationships is a large part of that and is often a first step toward understanding institutional culture. Community college presidents in Eddy's (2005) study found it was important to "look, learn, and listen" (p. 12) when first taking on a leadership role, as president or otherwise.

Institutional culture is also important in promoting racial equity on campus. While much attention has been given to campus racial climate, Museus and Harris (2010) argue that racial climate is insufficient to address racial/ethnic inequities on campus. They go on to illustrate the difference between institutional culture and campus climate. Specifically, climate refers to the *current* perceptions, understandings, and attitudes of campus community members. Culture, however, speaks to the values and beliefs that are deeply *embedded* in the institution through practices and policies. One might argue, therefore, that institutional culture is more difficult to change because of this embeddedness. Unfortunately, few studies look at institutional culture at community colleges (Orellana, 2019), and even more scarce are studies that look at institutional leaders' role in fostering or attempting to change institutional culture, particularly at community colleges. Still, one thing is clear: Creating a change in institutional culture is a long-term project and investment.

Understanding institutional culture and identifying necessary changes is critical for any college, particularly in terms of fulfilling the institution's mission related to transfer and credential completion. That said, it is also important to creating the necessary environment for a teaching and learning community for all members: administrators, staff, faculty, and students.

The CCSSE, instituted in 2001, is annually administered to community college students to better understand their specific experiences. Institutional leaders can use the tool to better understand the ways the college impacts students in terms of their engagement, their learning, the quality and frequency of their interactions with faculty, and the supports they receive on campus. In 2001, a companion survey was sent to faculty at the institutions where the survey was previously administered to students (McClenney, 2007).

While some of CCSSE's major findings include issues that are relevant to institutional leadership in understanding the campus environment from the student perspective (e.g., CCSSE shows a significant difference between the ways students and faculty perceive faculty practices), it has been criticized for including indicators of "student effort" without considering "intercultural effort" (Dowd et al., 2011). In other words, "An inclusive instrument would have the ability to measure all aspects of 'student effort' including latent qualities such as efforts to counter the effect of marginalizing experiences within the educational environment" (p. 22). This would improve college leaders' understanding of institutional effectiveness. Otherwise, racialized beliefs held by some faculty and staff may be reinforced.

Dowd et al. (2011) further argue that without understanding "intercultural effort" on the part of students and practitioners, the college will miss important indicators of institutional effectiveness. Thus, leaders will miss appropriate solutions to concerns around intercultural interactions, discrimination and racialized belief systems, and racially biased practices. These issues have always been important considerations in higher education, even if not always recognized; however, the need for institutional leaders to take a closer look at these issues is long overdue.

Considering the racial and ethnic diversity of community college leadership is a step in that direction. The "AACC Competencies for Community College Leaders" (AACC, 2018) were developed, in part, to respond to the lack of racial/ethnic and gender diversity among college presidents and the benefits of diversity (Wilson & Cox-Brand, 2012). Wilson and Cox-Brand, however, questioned how women and people of color would "decode" AACC's competencies:

> They [AACC] describe leadership in terms that are both directive and participatory; they describe skills and knowledge areas needed for leaders. But they cannot replace mentoring and storied descriptions of leaders in the media and in research. Growing leaders at community colleges and leadership programs focused on the community college context will continue to be critical avenues for encouraging participation in leadership [by people of color and women]. (p. 82)

Thus, as the racial, ethnic, and gender diversity of community college presidents continues to increase, all members of the college—from the students to the board of trustees—must recognize that these factors, and the way race/ethnicity and gender intersect shape the ways people of color and women lead, which may be different than the ways white men, who have historically dominated college presidencies, lead. This impacts who is selected as president and who is successful in the position. And, ultimately, it speaks to the success of the institution.

Discussion Questions

1. Consider AACC's competencies of community college leadership. Which of these do you find most relevant to your work?
2. From your perspective, what makes an effective leader?
3. This chapter encourages us "to engage in a dialogue about an evolving leadership model." What does that mean for you? How would you apply these principles?
4. How do we move from transactional to transformational leadership?
5. What examples of transformational leadership can you identify, if any? What does it look like on your campus or other campuses at which you've worked or attended? If you haven't seen it, why do you think you haven't?
6. How do we build new "core buildings" without "gentrifying" community colleges and losing the core principles of the institution?
7. What is the significance of creating a culture of "by us, for us?" What does the phrase mean to you?
8. If institutional culture is harder to change than institutional climate, how difficult is it for an institution to create meaningful change?

PART TWO

STORIES FROM THE FIELD

Hence the President's Commission suggests the name "community college" be applied to the institution designed to serve the educational needs of the local community . . . Its dominant feature is its intimate relations to the life of the community it serves.

— President's Commission on Higher Education, 1947, p. 5

There are as many examples of colleges doing good work for students and community as there are community colleges. Middlesex and Northern Essex Community Colleges in Massachusetts were most significant in the economic and social redevelopment and renewal of Lowell and Lawrence; Eastern Maine Community College continues to provide hope for students and communities around Bangor after many of the mills of that region of Maine closed; South East Kentucky Technical College has been working with displaced coal miners in and around Harlan County; J.F. Drake State Community and Technical College in Huntsville, Alabama, is working with Athens State College to address Alabama's teaching shortage; San Diego Mesa College is also working with nearby colleges on their communities' teacher shortage; and none have done more with regard to civic learning and engagement than the Foothills/De Anza colleges. The list of good colleges doing good work for students and community is too long for a single publication. The following, however, are five stories from around the nation that showcase some of that work in a bit more depth. Based on personal visits with the leadership, faculty, staff, and students, each amplify the ways in which community colleges are building community and sustaining democracy one student at a time. Given our interest in colleges being anchors of democracy and society, we chose five public institutions representing geographic diversity. The five highlighted colleges capture some of the good work happening in different parts of the country, from the rural southwest to large and small metropolitan areas in the Midwest and the coasts. Given that approximately 72% of all Tribal Colleges are two-year institutions and nearly half of all Hispanic-serving institutions (HSIs) are two-year colleges, we thought it was especially important to feature them.

I called Randy Smith, executive director of the Rural Community College Alliance (RCCA), to talk about the concept of the book and our desire to tell the story of a rural college. I knew he was most knowledgeable about what was happening in rural communities and rural community colleges. It was important to visit with at least one rural college, and a RCCA college would be great.

GCC was a member college, and Randy had come to visit our college and community. I was also on the board for a term or two. According to their website,

> The Rural Community College Alliance (RCCA) helps its member institutions serve the 89.3 million people who reside in rural America. We seek to promote a more economically, culturally, and civically vibrant rural America through advocacy, convening, leveraging resources, and serving as a clearinghouse for innovative practice, policy, and research. (RCCA, 2021, para. 1)

"I love the idea of the book," he said, "and I know just the college." Randy then told me about CSC in Warner, Oklahoma, where "the community gave a ranch to the college." "Perfect," I said, "that's the kind of relationship between college and community that we are looking for. . . . We want to tell their story." Through email and then over the phone, I had the privilege of meeting and talking with President Ron Ramming about our book and CSC. He was all in. I had a date for the visit and air tickets to Tulsa.

It was time to learn more about Oklahoma, Tulsa, Warner, and Muskogee. The main campus of CSC was in Warner, and they had another campus in Muskogee. I had never been to Oklahoma and mostly heard of Muskogee because of music (Merle Haggard) and of Tulsa also from music (J.J. Cale, among others) and as a college sports fan (Golden Hurricanes). But I am ashamed to admit that I had no knowledge of the Tulsa Race Massacre. I needed to do some homework and learn about it.

It was more than a coincidence, I think, that I instantly became a fan of the HBO miniseries *Watchman* with Regina King. That TV show took place in Tulsa, Oklahoma, prior to, during, and long after the Tulsa Race Massacre of 1921. Although CSC was over an hour southeast and around 100 miles away, it was imperative that I learn more about that part of America's history before I flew to Tulsa.

The Tulsa Race Massacre occurred over 18 hours from May 31 to June 1, 1921. A white mob attacked residents, homes, and businesses in the predominantly Black Greenwood neighborhood of Tulsa. That attack was one of the worst incidents of racial violence in U.S. history and has up until very recently remained one of the least known. I was beginning to understand why

I knew too little about it. It was hard to find any news of the attack, despite the fact that 36 died, more than 800 people were admitted to hospitals, and as many as 6,000 Black residents of Tulsa were interned in large facilities, many of them for several days. Before I left Tulsa, I had to visit Greenwood.

If the intent of the massacre was to destroy the economic backbone of "Black Wall Street" in 1921, it sure seemed successful even as I just drove through in 2020. As it turns out, the attack on the economic foundations of Greenwood continued over time, an insight into the ways that systemic racism ravages communities over time. Like the decisions in so many large and small cities around the country, the interstate highway system ran right through the Black community of Greenwood.

My all too quick visit to Greenwood and the increasingly vibrant downtown Tulsa brought an even brighter light to the work of and need for community colleges in the communities of America. There are far too many neglected communities in rural America, in urban America, in the South, and in the North where the economic engines have run out of fuel because the educational pipeline in the United States has not received as much attention as the gas and oil pipelines running through them. CSC in Warner Oklahoma was doing its part to contradict that economic and social narrative. My visit to CSC was affirming, uplifting, and a wonderful example of all that a passionate and dedicated faculty and staff with good leadership can accomplish with and for the community it served. Democracy was being strengthened in rural Oklahoma because the community that CSC serves was being strengthened, one student at a time.

I could have stayed in Tulsa longer. My hotel had a rooftop bar that I didn't get a chance to visit. The downtown had more than a few places to hear good music and eat good food that I didn't get to, and I always learn a lot about a community, a town, or a city just by walking it. Oh well, next time. I do want to get back to Tulsa, where good people are hard at work doing good things for good people. Isn't that a song, "Gotta Get Back to Tulsa?" Was that Bob Wills or is it Ray Benson? Okay, we are on to the next college.

Soon after my return, Tara and I talked about the importance of visiting and telling the story of an HSI for the book. We discussed a few colleges. I thought it would be helpful to reach out to Carlos Santiago, commissioner of higher education for the Commonwealth of Massachusetts, for his insight. Tara agreed.

Santiago joined the Massachusetts Department of Higher Education in April 2013 as the senior deputy commissioner for academic affairs. Santiago had served as chancellor of the University of Wisconsin-Milwaukee (UWM), provost and chief operating officer at the State University of New York (SUNY) at Albany, and professor of economics at UWM and SUNY Albany, earning a PhD in economics from Cornell University. Santiago is the author or coauthor of six books and has published dozens of articles and book reviews, of which many focus on economic development and the changing socioeconomic status of Latinxs in the United States. On two separate occasions, in 1996 and 2011, Carlos was named one of the 100 most influential Hispanics in the United States by *Hispanic Business* magazine. I knew he would be helpful, and he was.

Soon into my visit with the commissioner, Santiago said, "I have just the college." He went on to talk about Hostos Community College in the Bronx, an HSI by design and purpose from inception. He told me, "I worked with Félix V. Matos Rodríguez, the college's past president and current chancellor of the CUNY system when we were both in Albany." Santiago added, "I have very high regard for Félix." He then took time to tell me about Eugenio Maria de Hostos, whom the college is named after. He told me that "Hostos was a Puerto Rican educator, sociologist, lawyer, writer, and political force for independence and liberty." Santiago then agreed to reach out to Chancellor Rodríguez on my behalf. Within a few days, emails back and forth, and a telephone conversation, I was invited to visit with President David Gomez at Hostos Community College on the Grand Concourse of the Bronx—the South Bronx.

Although I grew up in Miami, Florida, I spent many summers of my early years with family in Queens and in Brooklyn. I loved New York City (NYC) as a child, especially when riding with my uncle the cab driver through the streets of Manhattan. I still love it to this day, especially on weekends. The energy is both overwhelming and intoxicating at the same time. That said, I really did not know the Bronx well. As a card-carrying citizen of Red Sox nation, I had a particular disdain for Yankee Stadium, which is in the Bronx, and within eye sight of Hostos Community College. But off I went nonetheless.

The idea of a pandemic was nowhere in my thought process on February 9, 2020, as I drove across Massachusetts, down through Connecticut to NYC, to visit Hostos Community College. I checked into the hotel in the Upper West Side of Manhattan late in the afternoon. The front page of the *Boston Globe* that Sunday morning was far more focused on the upcoming New Hampshire primary than the coronavirus. There was one article asking the question of whether the tourism industry might be negatively impacted if there were a decline in the number of visitors from China; but for that, not a mention. I found the same as I read *The New York Times* that afternoon; again the focus was on the Democratic presidential primary. Although we all had been hearing about some aspects of the virus in China, I dare say that very few, if any, of the people I talked to as I checked into the hotel, sat next to at the crowded coffee shop that afternoon, or rubbed elbows with at the restaurant that evening for dinner had any clue that NYC was about to become the epicenter of the devastation from COVID-19. I certainly did not.

I wasn't at all concerned about shaking hands with the students, faculty, and staff I met at Hostos the following day. While there were plenty of hand sanitizers around the campus, there was no way in the world that the good people of that college could see that by mid-March their campus would be closed to students because of the coronavirus. I drove the 5 hours home that evening listening to music, news, and sports talk radio. Still, there was no real focus on the impact of COVID-19.

Soon after my return, I read the headline that Harvard University announced it was closing its campus and moving all classes online for safety reasons. Students were told to leave their dorms and head home. Although I found everything that is good and right about education at Hostos Community College during my visit just a few days earlier, and having left with an incredible sense of optimism, the pandemic of 2020 was about to grip the world and wreak havoc on our nation.

Because of the pandemic of 2020, I did not have the opportunity to visit GRCC, Diné College, and Berkeley City College in person. Instead, those visits, found in chapters 8, 9, and 10, were virtual. Yes, it was more accessible. Yes, it was far more affordable. However, I did not find it nearly as informative or rewarding as an in-person, face-to-face, see-and-feel visit. Those were some of the same sentiments expressed, alongside many exceptional comments in the Zoom meetings, with the students, faculty, and staff of those colleges. What follows are my reflections of an imaginary/virtual drive from Boston to Berkeley, visiting each college, made possible by Google Maps and Google Earth.

I left Boston mid-morning heading west on the Massachusetts Turnpike. I thought about the final scenes of the 1997 movie *Good Will Hunting*, filmed at Bunker Hill Community College, MIT, and Harvard. Will, the main character, is driving west on the "Pike." The song "Miss Misery" by Eliott Smith is heard in the background. On the screen is the "Welcome to the Berkshires" sign on the north side of the highway between exits 3 and 2. Driving past that sign during my days working at Berkshire Community College felt like exhaling after a day of meetings in Boston. The landscape of rural Western Massachusetts would soften the edges of the city experience. Now, however, it was just the start of a virtual journey from Boston to Berkeley.

My first stop was Grand Rapids, Michigan. It took me 12 hours to travel those 836 miles on I-90, keeping to the speed limit most of the time. I listened to local radio stations along the way, opting for satellite radio when static was the only music I could find on the tuner. The corporatizing of media has taken the "local" out of most stations. It is harder to get a feel for community on radio these days.

GRCC is much larger than I had anticipated. The multibuilding campus is just a few blocks to the east of the Grand River and the Gerald Ford Presidential Museum. The college is pretty much at the heart of the city. If you were to fly over the college, as I did on a Google Maps drone, you would see the Peter and Pat Cook Academic Hall right across the street from the library and around the corner from the GRCC Learning Commons. The Phyllis Fratzke Early Childhood Learning Lab, Wisner-Bottrall Applied Technology Center, and the fairly new GRCC Calkins Science Center are just a few blocks away. The beautiful Fountain Street Church, Crescent Park, city museums, and Ferris State University are all within walking distance. GRCC looks like a major urban university. It certainly fills that space and need for Grand Rapids. The many names on the GRCC buildings suggest a robust development focus. More important, they also speak to the support that GRCC receives from the community it serves.

My visit to Grand Rapids was informative, and the welcome was warm. It was time, however, to depart for Tsaile, Arizona, home of Diné College, our nation's first Tribal College.

I headed out of Michigan just before sunrise, traveling west on I-40 and then I-44. The colors of the morning light were but a precursor to the beauty of Navajo Nation. I looked to the great Navajo artists I found in Google searches to better understand the land and environment of Diné College and their service region of Arizona. The passions of such Navajo artists as Tahoma, Begay, Nailor Sr., Gorman, and Yazz provided the images and the beauty of Navajo Nation as I Zoomed across America.

Arizona is 113,998 square miles and home to 7.2 million people. All of the New England states plus Pennsylvania would fit inside the "Grand Canyon state." There, out in the middle of that vastness, 22.5 miles from the nearest hotel, I found Diné. As I drove into the community, I thought about the lyrics of a Navajo wind chant I read about in William Least Heat-Moon's (1999) amazing book, *Blue Highways*:

> Then he was told
> Remember what you have seen,
> Because everything forgotten
> Returns to the circling wind. (p. 412)

Of all the college campuses I have visited over the course of my career, I thought Diné was the most interesting. It was built in the tradition of the Navajo culture. The circles within circles of the buildings and campus design speak to the interconnectedness that I later heard President Roessel speak of. My conversations with the students, faculty, and staff amplified the reality. My visit to Diné was all too brief. I left before I wanted to. There was a warmth of spirit there that was familiar yet all too distant.

I drove 950 miles farther west from Tsaile, Arizona, to Berkeley, California, for the last leg of my journey, staying "one hour ahead of the sun," as musician Steve Goodman once wrote. It took about 14 hours. I decided not to travel the routes that went through Las Vegas or Los Angeles, instead stopping overnight just off the highway in Bakersfield.

The last time I was in Berkeley was 1989. Professor and scholar K. Patricia Cross was teaching at the University of California (UC), Berkeley, and I was looking for the best program to pursue my PhD. That was the first time in my life I had the opportunity and privilege to choose a college not based on cost or proximity alone. Cross was kind enough to invite me for a day to visit a class and meet students of that program. I learned two things that day: (a) I was going to attend The University of Texas at Austin because it was a more applied/practitioner focused program, and (b) had I attended Berkeley as an undergraduate, I would still be there, as a bartender. Wow, what an exciting campus and college town!

According to Google Maps, it is about a 15-minute walk on Center Street from Berkeley City College to UC Berkeley. You pass the Berkeley Art Museum and a few good-looking coffee shops. If you detour just a bit you can enter the university through Sather Gate. The distance between the two colleges is just .7 miles. Yet, according to my conversations with students, the journey feels insurmountable, that is, until they enter the doors of the downtown building of Berkeley City College.

Berkeley City College was built in the heart of the city. On a map it looks like it is situated in the economic center of Berkeley, directly between Berkeley High School and the university. It seems purposeful, an almost perfect metaphor. Education and jobs, education and civic engagement, education and economic mobility, education and liberty, education and democracy—one building and yet so many powerful outcomes.

It was time to head back east. The drive back to Boston took me 45 hours, covering 3089.6 miles. I had thoughts of driving through New Orleans for some oysters, jambalaya, a visit to the Café Du Monde, and a large dose of life-affirming music, but I was ready to get home. Virtual reality can only take you so far.

What We Learned

We learned a great deal from the leaders, faculty, staff, and students at the colleges we visited for this book. From the Bronx to Berkeley, leadership, faculty, and staff were oozing with passion and commitment to their students and the ways in which education levels the playing field in the pursuit of social/economic justice and democracy. We also saw with great clarity that each college was tethered in service to its community. Each community's college would turn on a dime to meet community need, often doing so without having the dime. We found a wide range of differences in our visits, and at the same time some very common themes and values as well. Here are three key takeaways and commonalities:

1. *Community college faculty and staff are passionate about students and the open door.* They know their students and develop programs, pedagogy, curriculum, and wraparound services to help each student succeed. They understand the needs of first-generation students, students of color, and those who are food and housing insecure. They have learned about the challenges and successes of the academically underprepared, student parents, and the adult learner. Their expertise in teaching and learning is well informed by the loving understanding of students that are in the middle of life and not just preparing for it. All of the students we met with wanted a good job at good wages as a result of their education. In response, community colleges have developed programs for transfer in partnership with four-year colleges and programs geared to the local workforce, partnering with local businesses. Equity, inclusion, and diversity are shared cultural values, embedded in their day-to-day work. There was, in all colleges, a keen understanding and passionate commitment to the link between opening the doors of higher education and the sustainability of democracy.

2. *Community colleges' faculty and staff recognize the importance of "belonging" and "community" to student success.* With the AACC (1988) publication's definition of community in mind "not only as a region to be served, but also as a climate to be created," (p. 7), we found that college leaders, faculty, and staff know why and how to build and sustain a climate of community on campus. For all too many community college students, it is a first-time experience. College libraries were often a space for community building, but so too were fitness centers, gymnasiums, hogans, rodeo arenas, outdoor learning labs, student life areas, dining commons, tutoring centers, as well as art, music, and academic studios. College leaders, literally and figurately, walk the halls of their colleges with purpose, design, and authenticity, building community in every step. Education is, in the final analysis, a very human endeavor, and those colleges understood that. The students we met at those colleges talked passionately about

"community" and "belonging" as significant to their college experience. The colleges we write about model the community they want the world to become.

3. *Community college leaders are as active and engaged walking the halls of the community as they are walking the halls on campus.* The presidents we talked with are fully engaged in the social and economic development of the communities they serve. "Yes" is the default response to a request for community collaboration. They sit on local boards and committees with business, health care, and elected leaders working on community challenges. Each attend every community celebration that time allows, and even when time does not. College leaders open their college's doors to community conversations and community activities. They are approachable, engaging with members of the community while attending community events or shopping in the local markets. College leaders are visible and active in the betterment of community as a matter of practice and not just of theory.

5

CONNORS STATE COLLEGE

Even if you're on the right track, you'll get run over if you just sit there.

—Will Rogers

The hour-and-20-minute drive from Tulsa to the main campus of CSC in Warner, Oklahoma, was pretty direct, with signs and scenes along the highways that spoke to the transitions from city to country. From Lady Antebellum and Kenny Chesney to hometown favorites like Reba McEntire, Blake Shelton, and Carrie Underwood, the music on the radio was in harmony with every mile. That drive also felt a bit like time travel. It is not that you go back in time to an Oklahoma that you might have found in an old dusty black-and-white photo of an era gone by. Rather, you fast-forward into the future.

Rural America is under siege from a binary economy that uproots all too many jobs and young people, transplanting them to larger cities. Such is the case in Oklahoma. Although you can see the resulting vibrancy in Tulsa and Oklahoma City, those economic forces are causing a majority of "Sooners" to replant their flags in the two major metro areas of the state for the opportunities once found in rural communities. That demographic shift is as caustic to rural Oklahoma as any potential seismic shift that might lie just below the surface.

According to *The New York Times* article "Farm Country Feeds America, But Just Try Buying Groceries There," by Jack Healy (2019), "Farm towns . . . that produce beef, corn, and greens to feed the world are becoming America's unlikeliest food deserts as traditional grocery stores are forced out of business by fewer shoppers and competition from dollar-store chains" (para. 2). Their departure has left rural towns worried about how they can hold on to families, businesses, and their future if there is nowhere to buy even the basics. "About 5 million people in rural areas have to travel 10 miles or more to buy groceries, according to the Department of Agriculture" (para. 6). It's the new narrative for much of rural America.

Young folks are increasingly leaving those communities for greater opportunity; according to the U.S. Department of Agriculture's 2018 report on rural America, the migration out of rural towns and cities is resulting in a challenging downward spiral. Fewer people stay in the communities they grew up in, and fewer young families move into those cities and towns, downsizing the economies of scale. That change has a negative impact on everything from schools and business to health care, ranching, and farming. The downward demographic spiral also creates an even greater gap in the skills and workforce needed to fill the jobs that do exist in those now even smaller rural communities (Cromartie, 2018). Those are the significant factors you can see and feel as you drive around the communities served by CSC.

Students in rural areas have lower average rates of college enrollment and degree completion compared to nonrural students, according to a 2019 study conducted by UMass Amherst, published in the *American Journal of Education*. Only 18% of high school students seeking a college degree are from rural areas. Oklahoma data suggest that over 40% of the current and future jobs will require a bachelor's degree, while only 25% of the state has earned one. Being left out of the nation's economy runs akin to being left out of the nation's democracy (Wells et al., 2020).

You can't visit either campus of CSC without feeling the significance of the college in the greater community. Not only is it the second largest employer in the region, but it also provides the much-needed workforce for cattle ranching, nursing, and teaching. Students graduate from CSC with the requisite skills and knowledge necessary for family-sustaining jobs, and the community receives the workforce it needs. For example, according to President Ramming, about 40% of the teachers in the Warner school district are CSC alumni. He went on to say that according to the State Chamber Research Foundation 2019 report, CSC generated approximately $44.5 million in total economic impact for FY 2016. As a result, the communities that CSC serves then have an increased opportunity to slowly, and with sustainability as a goal, turn that downward spiral into a widening gyre of opportunity and hope. Graduates become more engaged and empowered citizens. Warner and Muskogee become more sustainable and stable communities.

I arrived at CSC about an hour before my meeting with President Ron Ramming with the intention of having a cup of coffee in the campus center. You can learn a lot about a college by visiting the campus center. As I entered the dining area, I found about three busloads of local elementary school students having lunch. I was sure it was because of my tie that they assumed I was on the faculty or staff, but I was greeted with high-fives by more than just a few of the children as I walked through to the food stations. They acted as if they knew me. As it turned out, I was greeted with that kind of welcome from everyone I met on campus; students, faculty, and staff alike. Community was a feeling at CSC as much as it was a group of people living in the same place. Later, the president told me that the connection and work with the local elementary schools to elevate the aspirations of those children was as important to CSC as Connors' Pell program at the local prison for educating and training the incarcerated. "You want to see real impact, Bob? Come to one of our graduations at the prison. Our first graduate is now a lawyer."

"Are you ready to see Connors State?" said the president with obvious pride. "You bet," I replied eagerly. Our first stop was at the college's horse barn, just down the street from his office. The large number of horse trailers and pickup rigs in front of that barn spoke to the number of CSC students who rodeo. That scene looked a little familiar to me, similar in some ways to the community skating rinks of New England filled with would-be developing Nancy Kerrigans and Bobby Orrs.

Across the road from the horse barn, the education building houses the agriculture program and its many awards, humbly displayed in the trophy cases on the first floor. President Ramming is as proud of the trophy for the 2019 National Champion Santa Gertrudis Bull as he is of CSC's National Junior College Athletic Association titles in men's and women's basketball. Pictures and trophies of the rodeo, softball, basketball, baseball, skeet shooting, agriculture, and student leadership teams are seemingly everywhere on campus, each team having built community and the resulting student success in every experience together. The president speaks with equal pride of the coaches, faculty, and staff who choose to stay at CSC, even as more pay and prestige beckon like a siren call. And so, he should.

With a majority of its 3,000 or so students commuting to one of its two campuses, close to 300 students live in the dorms on the main campus in Warner. Thirty-nine percent of CSC students are the first in their families to attend college. Almost 70% identify as female and about 30% as male. Seventy percent of CSC students attend part-time, and 30% attend full-time. CSC provides more than $2.25 million in scholarships and financial aid to its students. Approximately 50% of the current student body are people of color. About 33.6% of CSC students are Native American, most from the Cherokee and Muscogee Creek Nations. Beautiful Native American art is on clear display in the building where the president's office is, and which now houses a Native American cultural center.

Native Americans comprise only 1% of the U.S. undergraduate population; 17% continue their education after high school compared to 60% of the total U.S. population. Native American students are more likely to attend public colleges or universities versus private institutions of higher education, such as CSC or one of America's Tribal Colleges. In 2017, 27% of Native Americans attained an associate degree or higher, compared to 54% of white students. In 2000, 30% of Native Americans age 25 to 29 had attained at least an associate or bachelor's degree; that number fell to 27% in 2017. Native American students are less likely to have family members who have attended college (21% compared to 52% of white households), and 62% take out some kind of federal student loan, compared to 56% of white students.

President Ramming first came to CSC as a student enrolling in the college's agriculture program. After transferring to Oklahoma State University to earn a bachelor's degree, he came back to teach. "They must have confused me with another student or forgot who I was because they hired me," he said. President Ramming has not left since. He has learned, taught, and administered—but always he has led. His love of students, colleagues, college, and community was apparent throughout my visit. He knew students by name as we passed them on campus, whether it was a basketball player who blew out his knee, a skeet shooter who attended the president's leadership seminar, or the director of the nursing program who was a student in President Ramming's first class when he was a member of the faculty. It was clear that relationships and belonging matter to President Ramming. It was just as clear that students, faculty, and staff felt the same.

It was also apparent that President Ramming is as engaged *off* campus *in* the community as he is *on* campus *building* community. "You and I both know that you get pretty popular pretty quick in these positions at these colleges," he said to me. "They need you to serve on this board or that." And serve he does. John Dewey would be pleased to know that in addition to the many statewide and regional committees and boards, President Ramming has served on the local school and chamber of commerce boards, just to name a few. He is a fully engaged "community school" leader for sure.

"Can we head out to the ranch?" I asked. Driving the three-mile dirt road in President Ramming's truck toward CSC's 1,315-acre ranch gave me the time to hear from the president about how the ranch was "gifted" to the college. Apparently, there was a farmer who was more interested in cannabis as a crop than his watermelons or even his cows. To make a long story short, law enforcement agencies took the ranch, local folks got involved, and eventually they said, "Let's give the ranch to the college for their agriculture programs." Today CSC uses the ranch for its agriculture, cow ranching, and skeet shooting programs. The president also pointed out the many different types of grass found on the ranch and what cow ranchers think about each type. "Some are just not as good for cows as others," he said.

Mile after mile, acre after acre, the story unfolded like a made-for-cable TV docudrama. I especially enjoyed seeing the staircase concealed under a case that led down to the now defunct underground hydroponic marijuana growing area. "How did they discover this?" I asked. "There are stories," he replied with a smile and subtle chuckle.

After we explored the two man-made lakes on the ranch, President Ramming asked me, "Do you want to go see the students shooting skeet?" "Sure thing," I replied. The president sounded excited. The skeet shooting area was only about a quarter mile from the lakes, still on the ranch. President Ramming talked to me about the investment in the ranch, including the skeet area for the students, adding how much more could be done if the budgets were better. But mostly, he just seemed to want to talk to the students and the team coach, asking "How we shooting today?" Skeet shooting was and continues to be as significant a part of the community culture as cow ranching and farming.

According to President Ramming in his message posted on the CSC (2021) website:

> Connors State College has a long history of providing the people of eastern Oklahoma with access to higher education. Since seating its first class of seventeen students in 1908, the institution has grown into a comprehensive, multi-campus, two-year college that enrolls more than three thousand students annually. (para. 1)

There was no doubt in my mind that President Ramming understands that providing a first-class education is enhanced by building and maintaining first-class buildings and grounds. As I walked around both the Warner and Muskogee campuses, I could see that CSC truly gets how important it is that the college, in this rural and economically challenged community, send a message to all students, faculty, staff, and community that they deserve a first-class learning environment. Although underfunding is the new norm, President Ramming and CSC leadership worked hard to ensure that the development of the new building at the Three Rivers Port Campus in Muskogee, became the most recent example of the CSC commitment toward that end.

Although the Three Rivers Port Campus was built in 1995, its new building is the center of the CSC Nursing Program. The state-of-the-art nurse education building and simulation labs speak to an important and first-class nursing program. On July 8, 2019, CSC, Northeastern State University (NSU), Northeastern Health Systems, and Cherokee Nation came together to sign a memorandum of understanding and formally announce their ADN (Associate Degree in Nursing) to BSN (Bachelor's Degree in Nursing) to employment partnership. According to that memorandum, NSU will provide CSC space on the NSU Tahlequah campus to operate a satellite program of CSC's current Associate of Applied Science in Nursing Program. President Ramming said Connors is excited to work with the Cherokee Nation, Northeastern Health System, and NSU to extend their nursing program into Cherokee County. In the CSC (2019) publication "Connections," he said, "We believe this partnership will prove to be an excellent example of how the public, private and tribal sectors can work together to address critical workforce needs" (p. 3).

Steve Turner, NSU president, added that the partnership is a perfect example of public higher education's ability to respond quickly to community workforce and health care needs. "Future graduates of this nursing program will provide direct patient care to those with heath challenges and will bolster the number of health professionals in the area," Turner added. "The financial support provided by the Cherokee Nation and Northeastern Health System is key to the program's success. NSU is pleased to work with Connors State College to increase the number of nurses in Green Country" (CSC, p. 3).

Cherokee Nation and the Northeastern Health System have each agreed to fund a faculty position for the new satellite nursing program. The partnership will expand current nursing education and workforce opportunities for CSC and NSU students, improving the overall health and well-being of the citizens of Cherokee County, the Cherokee Nation, and patients of the Northeastern Health System.

Cherokee Nation Principal Chief Bill John Baker said, "Increasing options for health care education in northeast Oklahoma means we are able to help fill the workforce needs of the future and allow young people the ability to compete for jobs here at home." He added,

> Producing skilled nurses with an associate degree from Connors State and bachelor's degree from NSU addresses the health care shortage we see today across rural Oklahoma and makes it easier for nurses to advance their degrees. Cherokee Nation is proud to play a major role in this unique and forward-thinking collaboration of tribal, community, and higher education institutions. (CSC, 2019, p. 4)

President and CEO of Northeastern Health System Brian Woodliff said NHS is proud to participate in this collaborative effort to address the growing demand and shortage of nursing:

> Students will have what the community has long needed, a local program to begin and finish their nursing curriculum and clinical rotations thanks to participants. We appreciate the leadership and partnership of Connors State College, Cherokee Nation and Northeastern State University. NHS intends to be the employer of choice for many of the students to care for a community for years to come. (CSC, 2019, p. 4)

It was pouring down rain by the time we left the CSC Three Rivers Campus. Randy Smith, executive director of the Rural Community College Alliance, who introduced me to the good work of President Ron Ramming and CSC, and I were headed for dinner. According to their website:

> The Rural Community College Alliance (RCCA) helps its member institutions serve the 89.3 million people who reside in rural America. We seek to promote a more economically, culturally, and civically vibrant rural America through advocacy, convening, leveraging resources, and serving as a clearinghouse for innovative practice, policy, and research. (Rural Community College Alliance, 2021, para. 1)

Our time together that evening provided Randy and I with the opportunity to discuss the current challenges to rural America and just how significant community colleges are to the sustainability of those communities.

CSC is not only meeting the mandates of its mission, it was clear to me that CSC is in fact an anchor of democracy for the students and community that they so passionately serve.

Reflections

This chapter further illustrates the unique challenges that face rural community colleges. CSC, as a part of a larger rural community, faces struggling farmers and younger generations of residents leaving the community. Remaining jobs often go unfilled as a result. The community needs CSC. Founded as an agricultural school in 1908, it provides the community with the workforce it needs in teaching, health care, and cattle ranching.

CSC is one of three colleges we highlight without the word *community* in its name. It is interesting to note, however, that CSC is not a community college that dropped *community* from its name. On the contrary, the word was never a part of their name, not when it was accredited as a two-year college in

1927 or when it absorbed Muskogee Junior College in 1962. Still, CSC is the region's second largest employer and plays an integral role in the community.

In chapter 1, Bob specifically talked about the importance community colleges have to rural communities. Community colleges, including Tribal Colleges, serve not only the students who enroll in their courses but the entire community, as they are often the economic, cultural, and social centers of many rural neighborhoods across the United States. In these cases, they may be the only option for educational, cultural, and recreational opportunities for residents of all ages (Miller & Kissinger, 2007). Rural and urban two-year colleges are vital to their communities' economic and workforce development.

One important example of this is CSC's Second Chance Pell program. In 2016, CSC was one of three colleges in Oklahoma and one of 67 across the country to pilot this federal program that allows those who are incarcerated to receive Pell grants to take college courses. Although CSC has offered courses in prisons since 1997 and was accredited to provide degree programs there in 2000, students were not eligible for Pell funding. Pell grant eligibility allows CSC to offer more classes at two prisons near campus. The program also allows more students to near full-time status.

Founded in 2015 under the Obama administration, the Second Chance Pell program is now offered at 130 colleges and universities in more than 40 states and the District of Columbia. Two thirds of institutions with Second Chance Pell programs are community colleges. The program fits well with CSC's mission as it is designed to assist those who are formerly incarcerated to earn a credential (certificate, associate, or bachelor's degree) and find employment. In just the first 2 years, CSC's program more than doubled its enrollment and awarded 18 associate degrees to students in the program (McNutt, 2018). Given the institution's long history of serving those incarcerated and the impact of the more recent Second Chance Pell program, it is clear why the president was so proud to tell Bob about the program's first graduate who went on to be a lawyer.

CSC also maintains its commitment to serve two communities on two campuses. The college is an example of a "first-class education" with "first-class buildings." Like GCC it also emphasizes belonging and relationships on and off campus. CSC's collaborative intercollege nursing program is one outcome of those relationships. The collaboration shows not only ways community colleges and higher education in general respond to the needs of the community, but in this case it is a unique partnership between public, private, and tribal sectors that will increase the number of nurses in the region. Thus, the partnership is a direct response to health-care shortages in the area.

What is also important to note about CSC is the racial and ethnic diversity of its students, specifically that 33.6% of their students are Native American. This is particularly high for an institution of higher education that is not a Tribal College,[1] given Native American students represent approximately 1% of the student population of most U.S. colleges and universities. The presence of Native American cultures was clear throughout campus, which is an important demonstration of community, relationships, and belonging. Additionally, Native American students' representation is higher at CSC than the towns where CSC campuses are located, including Warner (0.77%) and Muskogee (12%), suggesting CSC's reach into the community is wider than its immediate surroundings. It is not surprising then to note that CSC has been awarded a Title III grant from the federal government since 2014 to strengthen their institution. The college has focused on (a) developing quality online courses and (b) improving Native American students' success. CSC is also home to the Native American Success and Cultural Center, which holds a computer lab, language repository, and study rooms for members of the college community and the general public. The center also maintains a collection of Native American art. This center is clearly an asset to the college and its surrounding communities.

Discussion Questions

1. How important is it to a state to have community colleges in rural communities?
2. With so many college graduates leaving rural communities, what is the role of the community college in sustaining the communities in which they are located?
3. What is equitable representation? In what ways should a community college reflect their surrounding communities?
4. As institutions of higher education are increasingly stratified, how important is it for community colleges and four-year universities to collaborate, as CSC is doing with their intercollegiate nursing program?
5. What's in a name? How important is it for community colleges to have *community* in their name? What do they lose? What do they gain?
6. How does a higher education program in prisons benefit the community? How does it benefit the college?

Notes

1. CSC did receive a Title III Native American Serving Nontribal Institution (NASNTI) grant in 2016.

6

HOSTOS COMMUNITY
COLLEGE

*Ideas are born, they struggle, triumph, change, and they are transformed: but is there a dead
idea which in the end does not live on, transformed into a broader and clearer goal?*

—Eugenio Maria de Hostos

I am not sure if it was a perfect symbol, an outstanding metaphor, or just the physical embodiment of a core value, but there it was, a bold and majestic bridge over the Grand Concourse connecting Hostos Community College to the community it serves in the South Bronx. My guess is that is exactly what the Puerto Rican community had in mind in April of 1968 when they petitioned, okay that might be a bit understated, when they demanded a community college in their community. Those Puerto Rican and other Hispanic leaders understood the need for, and the long-term importance of, a college in the community. That is why the college is named after Eugenio Maria de Hostos, a Puerto Rican educator, sociologist, lawyer, writer, and political force for independence and liberty. You can feel the passionate commitment to justice, liberty, and equity that Hostos the man wrote about in Hostos the college's classrooms, offices, labs, and especially on that bridge that connects to the community.

President David Gomez was in Albany on the day of my visit doing what all community college presidents do during the budget cycle. His advocacy for the needed resources was visible in the buildings, grounds, and faculty, and especially in the eyes of the students. The pride and passion of the people of Hostos were palpable. President Gomez was most gracious to travel back those 2.5 hours just to meet with me—gracious, but not surprising. It clearly doesn't matter to President Gomez whether you are a legislator in Albany, the borough president, a community leader, a member of the faculty, or a student whom he might meet riding the train

106

to and from the college; it was clear that the president loves Hostos, and he very much enjoys talking about it.

As our conversation flowed from topic to topic, President Gomez told me the story of a nursing student who graduated decades earlier. Like so many students at Hostos, she was a single mom of Puerto Rican descent, eager to make a better life for herself and her daughter. Celina Sotomayor went on to work at one of the hospitals in the Bronx. More important than the desire for a better job at better wages, she wanted to make sure her daughter understood the power of an education.

Fast-forward to about a year or so ago, President Gomez was welcoming a group of elementary school students to the college. He told them that Hostos Community College was a "magical place." He then introduced Supreme Court Justice Sonia Sotomayor. Her first words to the group of children were that Hostos was indeed magical. She went on to talk about how her mother, Celina, graduated from the college in the nursing program. I teared up as I heard President Gomez tell that story. Those tears of joy were also in response to the stories I had just heard from students only a few hours earlier. Celina's story was not unlike the stories of current Hostos students.

Of the five students I met with, three were single moms. All said that they are going to Hostos not just to get a better job. "[I want to] show my son how important an education is," said one student. "When I'm writing or doing some math assignment, even though my baby is in a crib, she knows that it's homework time," said another. "Playtime comes later, and my daughter understands that." There it was; there was the magic. From Celina Sotomayor to the students of Hostos today, the pathway to generations of a better life, a more empowered and engaged life, was through the doors of Hostos Community College. It was just as those Puerto Rican advocates had hoped for in 1968, and just as Eugenio Maria de Hostos had written about: lives were changing for the better because of the college, families were growing stronger, and even a Supreme Court Justice was in the making.

Those pathways to success are not easy at Hostos. The faculty I met with talked about the wraparound services that are offered in response to the challenges and "baggage" that so many students bring to the college. For example, about 78% of the students who enter the college are identified as underprepared for college-level work according to the Accuplacer assessment. The developmental education challenge at Hostos is as significant as any college in America.

The fact that the South Bronx is the poorest congressional district in America was not lost on me throughout my visit. The scent of smoke from the poverty that burned the Bronx is still in the air. That is part of what makes Hostos so "magical." No sleight of hand, no pixie dust, and no elixirs were going to transform the lives of students from such poverty, just hard work—hard work, passion, intelligence, leadership, community support, resources, and a whole lot of heart. As those "Damned Yankees" once said, "You gotta have heart, miles and miles and miles of heart." You can feel all of that at Hostos Community College.

Vice President Cruz grew up in the South Bronx not far from the college. He remembers the rubble of fallen housing all around his block, and he remembers the "Decade of the Fires." He referred to T.S. Eliot's poem "The Waste Land" when talking about the community that Hostos serves.

Yet now, all around the college, in fact all around the Bronx, you can see new building after new building. Some talk of opportunity, while others are talking about "the last stand for real community for these people." Whether you call it development or gentrification, it is clear that the Bronx, including the South Bronx, is changing. One of the many outcomes of Hurricane Sandy was that many learned that the Bronx is the only borough of NYC that is above sea level. Developers also saw that property value in the Bronx was very low in comparison to Brooklyn, Queens, and certainly Manhattan. So, as the hurricane forced people to look for new addresses, many have invested in residential, business, and industry development. "But where will these folks go?" I asked Julio Pabon, long-time community leader. "That's a good question," he responded. "After many years of community organizing, I have learned that the best strategy is to work *with* people to advocate for what we need, and we most definitely need to protect and advocate for these people." He added, "I guess some will move north, because they won't be able to afford the neighborhoods of NYC."

That, however, is not the case now. Over 7,000 students travel to Hostos every day. Each of the students I talked with were taking public transportation from home to Hostos. I thought about what it says when a student takes two trains and a bus to get to college every day and then two trains and a bus to get home. Of course, paying for that transportation is one of the barriers to student success that Hostos has had to deal with over time. Getting Metro cards in the hands of their students is a part of the support Hostos provides; childcare, a food pantry, and access to mental and physical health services add to that list.

Early in the college's history, most of the students were Spanish-speaking adults of Puerto Rican descent. Today, Hostos students have roots all over the world, Africa, South America, Central America, and the Caribbean just to name a few. All the students I talked with, regardless of where they came from, spoke of Hostos as "family and community." One student said that she checks in with the people in the EDGE program every day. "They are like family to me. I just stop in and they shout out, 'How are you doing today?' According to the Hostos website, CUNY's EDGE Program at Hostos is

> a partnership between the New York City Human Resources Adminis-tration (HRA) and the City University of New York. CUNY EDGE is dedicated to helping CUNY students who are receiving public assistance achieve academic excellence, graduate on time, and find employment. (Hostos Community College, n.d., para. 2)

"They all make me feel like I belong here," said another student when talking about the college. The truth is that Hostos is family and community for the students I talked with.

The college and its faculty, staff, and programs provide students a great deal of what so many families are able to provide the less at risk in our society. The courage, stamina, and heart of the students I met with was inspiring. One student boldly stated, with a wonderful bit of sass I might add, "I'm a spider not a chameleon." "I don't blend in all that easy," she added to clarify. "I want to lead and change things for the better, not just blend into the background." Another student told me she was born in the Bronx, had to move to Florida, and then came back, now living with extended family just to attend Hostos. Another student said that he first attended a different college. He wanted to be an engineer. "I didn't like it at [four-year college], and I didn't think they liked me." "I don't feel that here. People treat me with respect." He lived the closest to the college and only had to take one train. "I changed my major, and now I am in food service," a program that is tied directly into the ecosystem of the community. "They get me here," said yet another student with all the students in the room shaking their heads in affirmation. "How so?" I asked. "When I first came to Hostos and looked around I saw people just like me. I feel like I belong here." Another added, "I saw students, faculty, staff, and posters on the wall that all looked like me." "I feel like everyone here really understands who I am, because they are just like me." All the students added with emphasis, "Me too!"

Hostos has developed a rather significant student leadership program. VP Nathanial Cruz told me of the connection of the Hostos program and the student leadership program at West Point. Hostos is the only community college involved in that program. "Thirty percent of our students vote in student government elections," said the VP when discussing the level of stu-dent engagement. When I asked faculty if they see that same level of student engagement out in the broader community, they responded with the many names of alums and many stories of elected officials, business leaders, and community organizers who got their start at Hostos. "But let me just say," said one member of the faculty, "even if our students don't get that kind of notoriety, I can tell you that each are successes in the ways in which they live life." The point is well taken: It is hard to measure the full impact of an education. When talking with VP Cruz, he told me, "I saw the movie *American Gangster* a few times. I kept thinking that those were the alternatives for our students if they didn't come here."

"I was sick for a couple of weeks last year," said a student. She added, "I couldn't get to my classes. I would get a call from people at the college saying 'How are you doing?' Can you believe that? They called me at home, like I was their family or something. And they pushed me to show they cared about me. Family, belonging, community, relationships, caring, learning, jobs." Those are the words that I heard most over the course of my time with the students. I saw President Gomez's eyes fill as I told him what students had said. Those words by students, those outcomes, that commitment by faculty, and the president's reaction are tied together like a ribbon in the sky.

The student body at Hostos has changed from primarily Spanish-speaking adults to a more diverse student body shaped by the changing demographics of the South Bronx. The current student data on the college website suggests that enrollment at Hostos is 7,148, 66.2% of who identify as female and 33.8% male; 54.9% attend full-time while 45.1% attend part-time. White students make up 1.9% of the student population, 22.2% Black, 58.9% Latinx, 3.1% Asian/Pacific Islanders, 0.06% Native American, and 13.3% other/unknown. More than 66% of Hostos students live in the Bronx, 4.9% in Brooklyn, 3.5% in Queens, 0.1% in Staten Island, and 1.4% in Westchester; 4.7% report being foreign, and 2.1% are listed as unknown/other. Nearly 69% are U.S. citizens, 21.4% are permanent residents, 2.1% have student visas, and 0.1% have a temporary visa, while 7.7% are listed as unknown/other. Today, 10.6% of Hostos students are under 18 years of age, 36.1% 18–21, 17.8% 22–24, 16% 25–29, 16% 30–45, and 3.2% over 45, the average age being 24.9. Forty-five percent of Hostos students graduate with an Associate of Arts degree, 37% with an Associate of Applied Science degree, 16% with an Associate of Science degree, and another 16% with a certificate. Students graduate from Accounting, Early Childhood Education, Engineering, Nursing, Radiology Technology, Dental Hygiene, Community Health, and Criminal Justice programs, just to name a handful. Liberal Arts and Sciences is by far the largest major program, with 250 students in the last graduating class. Hostos graduates are the nurses, police officers, dental hygienists, teachers, artists, small business leaders, community organizers, and first responders of the Bronx.

Senior VP Esther Rodriguez-Chardavoyne, and the college's chief of security, took the time to give me a tour of the campus. I was struck by the condition of the buildings and the cleanliness. The floors looked like they were brand new, but they were far from that. "My compliments to your maintainers," I said. Rodriguez-Chardavoyne smiled and said, "Thank you; that means a lot to us. It's about respect for students, people who work here, and the community that visit us."

More impressive to me than the National Junior College Athletic Association (NJCAA) national championship trophies for men's and women's basketball that were on display in the trophy case was seeing that the gym was packed with students. The pool was also very busy; students were hanging out on the bridge (where most of the clubs and college information gets disseminated), and the café was bustling—and it was 3:00 in the afternoon! We stopped at the dental hygiene lab, which is open to the public by appointment. Rodriguez-Chardavoyne was clearly very proud of this program and facility. She told me how helpful the borough president was in getting the funds needed to build that lab as she pointed to his photo, one of the many of CUNY and community leaders who support the college that hangs just outside the president's office. That program and state-of-the-art lab was a beautiful example of how significant Hostos was to the community; students were learning, students were serving community, and the community was getting healthier. Professor Dewey would have been most pleased, a real-deal "community school."

Provost Christine Mangino came to Hostos to teach. She was teaching in the public schools and wanted to make the transition into higher education. With another degree and a search behind her, she arrived at 500 Grand Concourse in the South Bronx. Mangino found much more than a job; she found her purpose and a community. It is a shared story by the faculty and staff I met at Hostos, a journey of the heart. The spirit and morale of the professional folks was as uplifting as when I met students. There is a saying at the college that if you make it past "the test" (the first few years at Hostos) you will stay forever. The provost told me, "I have never been anywhere where the faculty hug so much." So, as the faculty came into the meeting to talk with me, I had to laugh out loud because Charles, Sonia, Hector, Fabian, and Raymond greeted each other with a hug. How beautiful is that? Do you think those relationships might have something to do with students feeling that Hostos cared so much about them—*community, relationships, and belonging?*

One member of the faculty, originally from Spain, told me that when she was hired, she was told that her Hispanic origins would make her a wonderful role model. Sonia then said, "The opposite has been true, the students here at Hostos are *my* role models." The other members of the faculty and staff in the room all nodded their head in agreement.

Another member of the faculty, Hector Soto (2018), wrote a compelling paper about the work of the community college serving community and democracy. In "Implementation of a Civic Engagement Community Change Model by a Community College Through the Integration of Technology and Social Media as Strategic Element," Professor Soto states

> today the task of addressing those challenges goes beyond the college merely serving as an institution for the education of the underserved student. The college today, as a matter of equity, needs to go beyond the traditional methods of linkage with the community, for example, community-based practicums, and strive to serve as a focal point and engine for curative community change. The college needs to work collaboratively with the marginalized community to alleviate those conditions and circumstances that continue to plague it, and which make it more difficult for the college to attract and graduate its students. This college-community collaboration to mutually beneficial results for both parties should be founded on an enhanced pedagogy of service learning, with a focus on community change through civic engagement. (p. 2)

Members of the faculty I talked with spoke about their work in the Behavioral Sciences, Education, English, and Developmental Education programs, providing wraparound services and support for students with disabilities, and speaking about the importance and abundance of arts. But for the most part, they spoke with passion about a calling to something larger than a subject matter or special program—something larger than themselves. They were talking about the community college movement.

That's the thing about community college faculty and staff everywhere. If you attend an AACC conference you can feel it: thousands of community college people coming together from all over America, filled with passion and commitment, loving their students and teaching just a tad more than their disciplines. The faculty and staff I met with at Hostos in the South Bronx were oozing with that passion and love. The students and community they served were different from Greenfield, which are different from CSC and different from Grand Rapids, Miami-Dade, Southwest Texas, Denver, and so on. And yet the core values and commitment were so very much in common.

President Gomez told me that the favorite part of his day is when he arrives on campus, early each morning, before things speed up. Down in the foyer of the campus is a piano donated to the college for all to enjoy. He told me that a student will be playing on most mornings. One day it might be a baroque piece by Bach, the next day a different student might be playing a funky New Orleans jazz piece, and the next day another student might be playing the salsa sounds of the South Bronx.

The arts at Hostos are as much a connection to/for the community as job training or that bridge that crossed the Grand Concourse. The art that hangs on the walls of Hostos is a beautiful representation of the many cultures found in the college and community—as is dance, and especially music. Music is indeed the world's language, and it is heard all around the college. I was thrilled to see that commitment to the arts, as a major, as a bridge to the community, and as a statement that shouted out the importance of the humanities at a community college. And what a fit it is at Hostos. Artists in the community bring their art to the college, and students at the college bring the arts to the community; in fact, they bring it to the world. For the past 2 years, students in theater at Hostos were invited to perform at The Fringe in Edinburgh, Scotland. Some of the best artists from around the world are invited to that wonderful city to perform and participate in the world's art community. Talk about bridges to opportunity. I am not saying that another J.Lo or Lin-Manuel Miranda is in the making, but of course, who knows. That's the magic that President Gomez and CUNY Chancellor Félix V. Matos Rodríguez talk about when they talk about Hostos.

It was so very easy to like President Gomez from the minute you meet him. The longer I talked with him, the more respect I had for him as well. He is one of seven kids. He told me that two of his siblings didn't make it out of the streets of NYC, and the four others are very successful in their chosen fields. With his SUNY Albany and Columbia degrees nowhere on display he said, "I am the least smart of my parent's seven children, believe me." The president began his career at Hostos as a member of the faculty, then left for a while to work at another CUNY college. He was recruited to return, this time as president. His pride and passion for Hostos was seen in his eyes and in all of the wall hangings in his office.

President Gomez announced his retirement to the college community the week before my visit, ending a most significant and powerful 10-year run between he and now CUNY Chancellor Matos Rodríguez. In Bynner (1972), Lao Tzu stated, "A leader is best when his work is done and his aim fulfilled, they will say: we did it ourselves" (p. 46). President Gomez was most pleased when I told him that although the faculty and staff held him in high regard, I did not get the feeling that they thought the college would fall apart, roam rudderless without navigation, when he leaves. He told me it was the right time for him and the right time for the college. The good news is that even though President Gomez is leaving, the culture of that college was born of the understanding that education is the vehicle best suited for liberty and justice for all. That commitment and culture are found in the halls, classes, and people of the college. It is in the bloodstream and DNA of Hostos, a result of the empowering work of the community founders and not a top-down influenced initiative or strategic plan. "Hostos is an anchor institution in the South Bronx and that isn't going to change when the President changes," said Chancellor Rodríguez. President Gomez will be missed, and he will miss Hostos, but both will do just fine.

Leonard Covello was the principal of Benjamin Franklin High School in East Harlem during the Depression. He focused on the community as a starting point for learning. Covello believed that the school was a means for social problem-solving and for training students in effective democratic citizenship. He believed in "education for social living" and that the school had to be "the leader and the coordinating agency in all educational enterprises" because

> the surging life of the community as a whole, its motion-picture houses, its dance halls, its streets, its gangs, its churches, its community houses, its community codes of behavior and morals—these will either promote or destroy the work of the school. (Benson et al., 2009, p. 25)

Principal Covello never met President Gomez or visited Hostos Community College in the South Bronx, not all that far from the Benjamin Franklin School in Harlem. But I am certain that had he, Covello would be buoyed by the experience.

I could feel the presence of Covello, Eugenio María de Hostos, John Dewey, Jane Addams, Sonia Sotomayer, and especially those pioneering Puerto Rican activists throughout my visit at Hostos. President Gomez, the faculty, staff, students, and community were putting into practice every day the ideals and values each of those leaders spoke and wrote about a century earlier. It is powerfully apparent to me that Hostos Community College is meeting the mandates of its mission every day and strengthening democracy in the South Bronx, one student at a time. Everything that is good and right about education is happening at Hostos Community College.

Reflections

Hostos Community College is one of seven CUNY community colleges. Perhaps because of its location, Hostos demonstrates an unwavering commitment to racial/ethnic diversity, justice, and equity. This commitment was established from the very beginning when it was founded as an institution "for us, by us" due to the demands of Puerto Rican and other Latinx leaders who demanded a college to meet the needs of the South Bronx. In its charter year, Hostos admitted a little more than 600 students in 1970. Enrollment more than tripled in just 4 years. Today, more than 7,000 students representing a variety of cultures, languages, countries, and boroughs enroll while the college still maintains an enrollment of more than 80% Black and Brown students.

Being located in the South Bronx of NYC, Hostos must face the challenges that often come along with large urban areas. In Hostos's case, they are located in the poorest congressional district in the United States. Perhaps as a result, Hostos offers many wraparound services and high levels of developmental education courses. Nationally, 68% of students who began at a community college in 2003–2004 took at least one developmental education course within 6 years. When looking at race and ethnicity, these statistics go up to 78% and 75% for Black and Latinx students, respectively (Center for the Analysis of Postsecondary Readiness, n.d.).

Institutions that serve predominantly students of color and are federally designated as minority serving institutions (MSIs) have a long history of providing opportunities to students who might otherwise be excluded from higher education due to inadequate academic preparation throughout their K–12 education. Institutional leaders, faculty, and staff at MSIs are often quite responsive to student needs by providing holistic support and services and comprehensive developmental education courses. Hostos is clearly no exception as indicated by caring leaders, faculty, and staff.

The care is evident in the voices of the students when they talk about feeling respected, validated, and affirmed. These are key to success, for students who take developmental courses in particular (Parker, 2012). Student voices showed that faculty, staff, and administrators at Hostos demonstrated that Hostos is a leader in supporting students who take developmental courses in two significant ways (Parker, 2012):

- They demonstrated "a fundamental belief in human potential" (p. 11). Despite placement tests indicating a need for developmental or supplemental support, members of the Hostos community saw students as leaders, as indicated by student testimony and the student leadership program.
- They provided holistic support that saw students not just as students but as people. Thus, students received support not just in academics but also financial and social support as well. One student, for example, shared that when she was sick and unable to attend class, someone from the college called to ask how she was doing. She said it was like "family."

Indeed, *family*, *community*, and *belonging* were some of the most common words heard at Hostos, and their meaning is evident in the conversations Bob had with the president, faculty, and staff.

As evident at GCC with their Core building, Hostos leaders found it important to have well-maintained grounds and buildings. Their state-of-the-art dental lab, for instance, was a point of pride for all in the community. The lab, however, is also important for the larger community of the South Bronx. As students learned dentistry, they also served their communities by providing needed services to residents in the area. The dental lab is another example of the ways buildings and facilities tell those who go to school or work there that they matter. And by extension, they tell the communities of the Bronx that they matter.

Another example occurred during the early days of the COVID-19 crisis. While some colleges and universities initially turned down requests to provide help to their local communities, Hostos did not hesitate. The president permitted the use of their cafeteria to be the central distribution center to get more than 4,000 lunch boxes to veterans across the five boroughs of NYC. Other administrators mobilized to collect and distribute more than 1,500 personal protective equipment (PPE) to local health-care workers. Hostos also donated gloves and Tyvek suits directly to a local hospital.

As Bob pointed out in chapter 1, many community college faculty and staff find purpose in working at community colleges. Perhaps because of their collective purpose, Hostos is able to fulfill its mission and its commitment to their students and community. Together, Hostos, like other urban community colleges across the nation, replaces deferred dreams that often plague the nation's largest urban centers

> with a college and career success model founded on the objectives of a multiracial democracy. They are taking bold initiatives . . . in areas such as leadership, policy development, workforce development, community partnerships, curriculum and student services, campus-wide diversity initiatives, resource development, and new business and financial models. In so doing, they are reframing the very definition of "democracy's college." (Myran & Parsons, 2013, p. 11)

Hostos does this by committing and then recommitting to the students and communities they serve.

Discussion Questions

1. How important is it for an institution to maintain its founding mission and continue to serve the people it was designed to serve? What does an institution need to do it?
2. A Hostos student talked about being a "spider not a chameleon." The student went on to explain by saying they don't want to just blend into

the background. They want to lead. Students who are nurtured and made to feel valued can begin to see themselves as leaders—in part because they have a strong sense of belonging on campus. What factors contribute to a sense of belonging?

3. What does it mean to be a federally designated HSI? What are the specific obligations or responsibilities of such a designation? What *should* they be obligated to do?

4. What is unique about an urban community college?

5. Developmental education is a concern for most community colleges. What are some specific examples of ways Hostos recognizes students' potential and provides holistic support for students enrolled in these courses?

7

GRAND RAPIDS
COMMUNITY COLLEGE

Do we settle for the world as it is, or do we work for the world as it should be?

—Michelle Obama (2018, p. 118)

On March 10, 2020, just days before I was going to leave for Grand Rapids, Michigan, to visit GRCC, the governors of Massachusetts and Michigan declared states of emergency due to COVID-19. It wasn't until the 1st week of August that Tara and I had the opportunity to meet President Bill Pink face-to-face. It was a Zoom meeting. Bill was gracious to (re)invite us to visit, this time virtually.

We were talking about the book and GRCC when President Pink said, "Look folks, we have a great deal to be proud of here, but I need to just say up front that we haven't arrived yet; we are still on our journey. Of course, we will never get to that end place, but it's the journey that matters." President Pink did not want the chapter in our book to overstate the accomplishments of GRCC. It was not false humility. It was a real-deal leader talking about a commitment to the process of betterment.

President Pink went on to talk about the plans and goals for GRCC. "Our focus is to be relevant and responsive to ourselves, our students, and our community." In an open letter regarding the 2018–2022 Strategic Plan to the community, President Pink (GRCC, 2022) writes:

> We must be the place all people can turn to gain an education and career skills. Our efforts must reflect the challenges faced by the people we serve and the goals they strive to reach. We will continue to remove obstacles to success and ensure everyone has an opportunity to thrive . . . Our strategic plan is our roadmap as we move forward. Our commitment to these goals will be unwavering. (paras. 3–4)

The GRCC goals for 2018 through 2022 are teaching and learning, completion and transfer, equity, community impact, sustainability, and infrastructure.

Early on, President Pink told us that the City of Grand Rapids always shows up high on national rankings and has great data about the quality of life and the economic environment of the city, "but that data does not include everyone." He was referring to the economic gap and quality of life for people of color that exists in the city. He went on to say emphatically, "GRCC is vested in widening that circle, to include more in the wonderful Grand Rapids story." The goals for equity, relevance, and responsiveness were real.

At one point in the conversation I said to President Pink, "As difficult as it has been for all in America during the COVID and racism pandemics of 2020, can you imagine what the communities of our nation would be like were it not for the presence, leadership, and engagement of community colleges?" His response was clear, emphatic, and with passion: "You have no idea just how right you are."

President Pink, as an example of that impact, talked about GRCC recently deciding to move into an empty JC Penney in a neighboring community to Grand Rapids. "Transitioning an empty business building into a point of access of education is a powerful statement."

President Pink also shared a conversation he had with a community leader who said, "If X or Y college were to close, we would mourn the loss but carry on. If GRCC were to close, our community would be compromised." Relevant and responsive.

I heard that refrain about relevancy and responsiveness along with the authenticity of the college's commitment in all my conversations with faculty, staff, and members of the Grand Rapids community.

Brian Knetl, provost and executive vice president for academic and student affairs, reinforced that mantra by talking about all of the partnerships the college has with the Grand Rapids Public Schools (GRPS) and other K–12 schools, the four-year institutions that GRCC students transfer to, and the area businesses where students work.

Knetl added a third R: responsibility. "We have a responsibility to all of our students for the time they are here. . . . We want them all to succeed." Brian told me, "Students come to GRCC to attend our middle college; they come from the GRPS, they drive every day from the rural outskirts, and they are adult learners who come to reskill and retool and in our noncredit workforce initiatives. We work at relevancy, responsiveness, but we also work hard at being responsible to all who attend."

I asked Knetl, "What wakes you up at 3:00 a.m.?" He thought for a moment and said, "I worry about the students who are not coming here, who do not think they have access to the education, programs, and opportunities we offer. We need to work at reaching those people."

Faculty also talked about responsibility, responsiveness, and about the relevance of GRCC in our meeting. Professor Vicki Cooper, a native of Grand Rapids and an alum of GRCC when it was Grand Rapids Junior College, said, "We teach life skills in addition to the content of our courses." She tells all of her students, especially those in her developmental integrated reading and writing course, "You are adding roots and branches to your family tree. Roots deepen your ability to withstand the winds of change and the branches reach out, growing and developing in new ways."

One student told me, "I was very shy, not very confident in myself before I came here to GRCC. My GPA and SAT weren't going to get me into University of Michigan, so I moved to Grand Rapids and enrolled here. Right after my orientation I was asked if I wanted to work as a tour guide. I met so many people in that job. . . . I was given so many opportunities here at GRCC. I'm in the honors program now. I have learned that GRCC is what you make it. I think that is true in life as well. . . . GRCC developed me as person."

Professor Lauren Woolsey talked about the importance of affordable access to a quality education. Woolsey shared her own journey from the astrophysics labs and classrooms at Harvard to GRCC. "I can tell you first-hand that the quality of the learning experience here in Grand Rapids is every bit as good as what I experienced in Cambridge," adding, "our students are just as able, but they have far fewer resources than the students there. . . . It is so important to our students that they have access to this level of quality at an affordable cost." She added in closing, "This is definitely my home."

Victoria Powers, Trio Program coordinator, was a migrant worker from Mexico, having moved to Grand Rapids at an early age. "Being the youngest in a big family without money, I never thought about going to college. And to be honest neither did my parents. But my best friend talked them into it." Her friend told her parents, "This girl needs to go to college." "I'll never forget her for that," Powers said.

Talking about her experience at a local university Powers said, "I truly was a stranger in a strange land when I arrived at [university]. It was a total culture shock." She went on to discuss what life was like as a first-generation person of color on a predominantly white campus. "I think those are just some of the reasons why I understand our students and have such high regard for them."

Powers learned her passionate commitment to social justice watching her parents help other migrant workers with paperwork and health-care issues. "I love my work in our Trio program. . . . I get to do what I love most—every day, teaching students how to learn and helping students build skills that will last them a lifetime."

Echoing the words and footsteps of Powers, a student, also from a Mexican farm-working family, talked about how important her role is in the family: "Staying home was comfortable and easy. But, GRCC is like a second home to me now." She went on to say, "My mentor in the Trio program pushes me out of my comfort zone sometimes, like when she pushed me to apply to the University of Michigan summer program. . . . I looked at the number of people who apply and who get it; I thought there is no way I will ever get into that program."

She paused and her eyes filled, "But I did; I got in. . . . It was an amazing experience, and I became a leader there." She added with emphasis, "The people in the Trio program mean so much me; they are all like family."

When talking about relevancy and responsiveness and responsibility, Professor Jermaine Reese told me, "I was a police officer in Flint assigned to a local high school. I wanted to keep kids out of jail more than I wanted to lock them up. . . . That's how I got hooked on education." Reese was an athlete at Eastern Michigan University until he got injured. "I know what it's like to have a dream crushed. But here at GRCC we encourage our students to re-dream. . . . Having a second chance in life . . . a clean slate, is something we talk about and students understand."

Reese eventually was able to combine his love for education, criminal justice, and law enforcement. "So many colleges were downsizing their programs, I am so thankful that was not the case here at GRCC. I wanted to make systemic changes in the way things were in law enforcement, teaching young police officers that they can make change is empowering for them. It is my responsibility to do that; it is our responsibility to the community."

The students I met told me how important campus life has been for them. One student started a gaming club at GRCC. "I pretty much stay here all day . . . sometimes till 6:00 p.m. . . . I don't just leave right after class." Another student said that his grandmother lives right near the college "so [he] visit[s] her sometimes."

And still another talked about theater at GRCC. "I want to pursue a career in movies. . . . My goal is to apply to USC or Howard. USC because it is right in the middle of the industry, and Howard because that is where Chadwick Boseman went. . . . I wanted to learn from him."

That student added, "My teachers and mentors here at GRCC opened my eyes to those possibilities." I look forward to calling the Civic Theatre, the oldest and grandest theater in Grand Rapids, to get tickets to that student's first grand opening. I have no doubt.

President Pink said, "It [being responsible and relevant to the community] has been that way at GRCC from the beginning. Our job is to live up to our reputation and then raise the bar." Professor Cooper couldn't agree more: "I think the community relies on us, expects us to live up to our responsibility to them; it is part of why I am honored to teach here."

Twelve years after Joliet Junior College, the very first junior college created by the leadership at The University of Chicago, Grand Rapids Junior College was established on September 21, 1914, after University of Michigan faculty passed a resolution encouraging the establishment of junior colleges in Michigan. Those origins are powerful in the definition of purpose and mission at GRCC.

The course offerings, based on University of Michigan offerings, were mathematics, history, rhetoric and composition, German, Latin, biology, and physics. Not unlike the beginning curriculum of Joliet, all the courses were focused on college transfer. Grand Rapids Junior College was the first junior college in Michigan, and transfer is still significant and core to the GRCC mission.

Forty-nine students graduated in the first GRCC class paying $60 per year for tuition. The following year, to encourage enrollment, tuition was reduced to $40 per year for Grand Rapids residents and $50 for nonresidents.

A total of 25,812 students were served at GRCC during the 2018–2019 year. The headcount for fall 2019 in the credit-bearing courses was 13,326. The proportion of students who were Michigan residents was 72%, while in-state nonresident students accounted for 27.1% and out-of-state students for 0.9%. One-year retention rates for beginning, degree-seeking freshmen from fall 2018 returning for fall 2019 was 53.9%, up from the previous year's 53.5%. Female students comprised 53.1% of the total fall population; 26.9% of fall 2019 students were age 25 or older. The average age of students was 23.7 years. Sixty-two percent of the student body identify as Caucasian, 15.4% Latinx, 9% African American, 4% Asian/Pacific Islanders, 3% two or more races, 1% Native American, and 6% unknown. The percentage of students from populations of students of color was 32%, up from 30% in fall 2018. The proportion of students who attended GRCC full-time for fall 2019 was 30.2%. The GRCC workforce development programs (training solutions, job training, and apprentices) enrolled 20,198, 176, and 768, respectively.

GRCC offers over 130 programs of study, including 39 workforce associate degrees and 37 certificate programs, including noncredit. GRCC has provided customized training to 57 companies through 227 classes, reaching 1,585 people. In addition, 427 companies were served through workforce training, continuing education, and professional development, reaching 18,613 community members in 2018–2019.

Twenty-eight percent of GRCC students transfer to Ferris State University, 25% to Grand Valley State University, 7% to Davenport University, 5% to Western Michigan University and Michigan State University, 3% to Central Michigan University, 2% to Calvin College, and 1% to the University of Michigan, Aquinas College, and Lansing Community College, while 23% transfer to other colleges around the nation.

In 2019 there were 240 full-time faculty, 156 clerical/secretarial/service/maintenance staff, 157 technical and paraprofessional staff, 33 executive/administration/managerial staff, and 13 skilled trades staff. There are 330 faculty and staff who identify as women, 307 identify as men, and 137 identify as students of color.

Like so many community colleges around the nation, GRCC first opened its doors in an old high school in downtown Grand Rapids. The college operated at Central High School from 1914 until 1924. In 1944 the college acquired the main building from GRPS. GRPS Superintendent Arthur W. Krause closed Davis Technical High School to save costs and gave the building to Grand Rapids Junior College. Today, GRCC is a vibrant presence, an anchor to the people and businesses in downtown Grand Rapids.

In 2012, GRCC collaborated with John Kennedy, then CEO of Autocam, along with other western Michigan manufacturers, to establish the Advanced Manufacturing Partnership to develop and sustain a stronger pipeline of manufacturing talent. Applicants accepted into the program start at $13 an hour while they attend classes for a two-year program paid in full by the company.

Upon completing the GRCC program and 8,000 hours on the job, machinists earn at least $17.50 an hour at a plant where the average annual income for an hourly worker exceeds $50,000. The company also picks up the tab if the worker wants to earn a four-year degree in fields such as engineering.

Kennedy told me, "GRCC is a gateway to education. . . . It opens doors to people who might not have access otherwise." He added, "We are not selling parts at our company; we are selling knowledge." Working with GRCC to provide free educational opportunities for his employees has paid off. Not only does he gain the educated workforce he needs to meet the mandates of his business's mission, but he also finds employees who are loyal to him and his company. "When I invest in them, they understand what that means, the core values behind the investment. . . . They appreciate what that says. . . . I don't worry about their loyalty." That public–private partnership is a win for students, a win for the company, a win for the community, and a win for GRCC. Kennedy declared, "Yes, GRCC is absolutely an anchor in this community!"

"My experience as a welder helps inform my understanding of my students," said Professor John Doneth. He talked about growing up in northern Michigan, not being clear about his direction alongside the very few opportunities he saw for himself. "Now I teach engineering, and I am overseeing our apprenticeship program here at GRCC. I get to help place these students where they can start earning $50,000 in their 1st year. . . . The companies in this community look to us first for the trained workers they need."

Doneth's face lit up when he said, "I took a pay cut to teach here after being an engineer, but I just love it . . . especially when I see my students in the grocery store, and they tell me how well things are going. I wouldn't trade that."

I could tell by his voice and look in his eye that he wouldn't, but it begs the questions, "Why is the income gap between university faculty and community college faculty so large? Why do community college faculty have to take a pay cut to teach?" I guess the reason must be because the challenge is so much more demanding.

Kathryn Mullin is vice president for college advancement and the executive director of the GRCC Foundation. She shared many stories with me about GRCC students and donors and said, "Development is a reflection of the relationship between the college and the community and a reflection of our relevancy and responsiveness."

Mullin shared her own story about the journey from a trailer park to the American Dream, adding "that is why I am so passionate about our work here at GRCC: I have lived the powerful impact of an education. . . . GRCC is providing a pathway for that journey for all in western Michigan."

She shared one particular example: "I like to get in the office early, before everything gets going. I was sitting there, and I could see the elevator door open and saw a student come out. He was clearly not happy. Turns out he was not happy that the offices were not open yet, and less happy to be at the college at all. I waved to him, 'Please come in.' He told me that he and his mother had just moved from Florida. He said, 'Mom told me that I had to come to this college; I don't want to be here and now I can't even register!'"

We sat and talked in my office for a while. We talked about education, I shared my story and what GRCC had to offer. He told me, 'I want to go back to Florida and go to college there,' adding, 'I don't know anyone here. But we can't afford it and momma said I have to be here.' I told him, 'You now know me, and I'm going to help get you connected here.' I got up and walked with him through the registration process."

"The next day his mother called me. She filled up with tears saying she had no one to help raise her son. 'No one has ever bothered to help us out.' 'Well now we are both his mom,' I said." That student did go on to graduate from GRCC, although he did find his way back to Florida.

With all that was moving forward at GRCC and in Grand Rapids, from March 2020 to August 2020, just 6 brief months, there was significant pain, hardship, and disruption. It will take decades to assess and unpack the magnitude of impact. There was no reason to believe the next 6 months would prove to be less challenging, especially so in higher education.

COVID-19 did not spare Grand Rapids and GRCC. The college provided food to students, PPE to the local hospitals, and opened its buildings, grounds, and parking lots to area health providers as needed. During that time the college went from 25% remote and 75% on campus to 75% remote and 25% on campus in the classrooms, labs, and studios.

Also, between March and August of 2020, 116 Black people were killed, including George Floyd and Breonna Taylor. The reality of Floyd's brutal strangulation came into our living rooms because a young woman had the courage to video that moment on her phone—in real time. America could not escape itself this time; a second deadly virus had to be confronted.

Like much of the nation, Grand Rapids responded by taking to the streets in protest. However, the response was especially emotional because Breonna Taylor, a 26-year-old African American emergency room technician killed by police in Louisville, Kentucky, in March—was a Grand Rapids native.

Just as COVID-19 had worldwide impact, so too did the killing of Floyd. When talking about the BLM protests taking place in the United Kingdom on CBS's *Sunday Morning*, Kehinde Andrews, professor of Black studies at Birmingham University said,

> It is interesting that a killing that took place 3,000 miles away has forced the UK to confront its racism. The BLM protests in America are not just about police brutality. They are also about economics, education, health care, and even the pandemic. The same is true here. Racism is not just an American problem, it's a world-wide problem and now we are having that conversation. (August 9, 2020, 10:21 a.m.)

Joseph "Joe" Jones, president and CEO of the Grand Rapids Urban League, Grand Rapids ward 2 commissioner, and clergy in the community, told me that "GRCC has been especially important as a convener for important and at times difficult community discussions," adding, "this is especially important right now, and I know that Dr. Pink and Dr. McNeely Cobham (GRCC's chief equity and inclusion officer) are committed to that role, on campus and in the community."

B. Afeni McNeely Cobham, an expert in race, identity, and culture in American higher education, was selected to serve as GRCC's chief equity and inclusion officer as part of the college's strategic equity goal. President Pink said in a GRCC (2018) press release:

> We're proud to have Dr. McNeely Cobham on our team to help us address the challenges locally, as well as regionally, around disparities in education and workforce. We are committed to being proactive in providing a high-quality education helping our students be successful in earning a degree, transferring to a four-year school or gaining career skills. This work makes our college stronger, and our community stronger as well. We've made great strides, but there is more to do. Dr. McNeely Cobham's expertise and passion will be invaluable as we move forward. (paras. 2–3)

McNeely Cobham is being asked to build on the college's existing efforts and develop a strategy championing equity and inclusion as another and important way to foster student success, employee and community well-being. She said she "works with students, faculty, staff, and community members to ensure that GRCC is a leader in equity and inclusion" (para. 5).

McNeely Cobham also oversees the Bob and Aleicia Woodrick Center for Equity and Inclusion, which focuses on educating and honoring the dignity of all people through opportunities such as the Institute for Healing Racism, student workshops, and the Latino Youth Conference and celebrations such as the Giants Awards.

"I will be focused on building upon and expanding GRCC's successful efforts in championing equity and inclusion," McNeely Cobham said.

She added:

> The CEIO will play an important role toward embedding principles of diversity and social justice into the bedrock of the institution. I plan to come alongside President Pink in carrying out this work through support and advocacy, assessment and strategic planning, recruitment and retention, and training and development. (para. 8)

The release goes on to state that

GRCC is one of west Michigan's most diverse colleges. There are more Latinx students than in any public college or university in the state, according to an Excelencia in Education's analysis, and the most African Americans in West Michigan, according to the National Center for Education Statistics. (para. 14)

McNeely Cobham talked about responsibility and relevance, and she talked about responsiveness when describing the antiracism work of her office and the college. "Creating the CEIO position and my office speaks to our commitment to students and the community." In the past few months Professor McNeely Cobham has created a series of town hall meetings for students and faculty. She has also convened conversations for and in the community. "They have all been courageous conversations."

McNeely Cobham told me, "Systemic racism is still hard to talk about for many people," adding, "it is brutally unfair that people of color are at the forefront of educating others. . . . There is not time for our own healing. . . . That said, who else but us?" She is also scheduling an online post-election town hall.

McNeely Cobham also talked about grace. "We won't heal anything until we address the wounds of hundreds of years. . . . People are shell-shocked. . . . We need grace for ourselves, and for others." Indeed, grace, compassion, and understanding would go a long way to heal many in our nation right now. There is no doubt that GRCC will be convening that conversation and modeling grace as well.

Reverend Jones added, "GRCC is an on-ramp for economic mobility, and they are committed to widening the circle of opportunity." Jones spoke with passion about GRCC providing that educational opportunity: "With access to education, a student has access to economic prosperity. . . . You can deal with racism just a bit better if you have money in your pocket."

One of the more recent and significant developments of that public–private partnership to "widen the circle of opportunity" in Grand Rapids has been the approval of Grand Rapids as a promise zone providing scholarships to GRCC. President Pink, Joe Jones, and Lisa Freiburger, vice president of finance and administration, all talked about the importance of the Promise Zone to students, college, and community. I can think of no better example of the ways in which the relationship between a community and its anchor educational institution elevates access and opportunity to a better life for all in its community.

The Grand Rapids Promise Zone Scholarship provides free access to GRCC's associate degree programs, job training, and certification programs for students who live within the city of Grand Rapids and graduate from one of the city's 24 public, public charter, or private high schools, starting with the graduating class of 2020.

Promise zones are designated areas in the state where public–private partnerships create community-based scholarship programs that offer high school graduates at least 2 years of free tuition.

A 2009 Michigan law allowed the creation of promise zones in communities with above average rates of childhood poverty. There was a cap of 10 promise zones. In November 2017, the number was increased to 15, allowing GRPS to apply for and receive a designation in 2018. With great support from the local Grand Rapids community, and with clear evidence of need, Grand Rapids was designated a promise zone.

The Michigan Promise Zones were inspired by the Kalamazoo Promise. Since 2006, anonymous donors have made it possible for graduates of Kalamazoo public schools to receive full tuition scholarships to any state university or community college in Michigan.

President Pink said, "It will be life-changing for so many students and their families. . . . We are removing cost as a barrier to getting an education." VP Freiburger added, "When you take away the financial barrier, we can all focus on the student's success with even greater impact."

Although I would have preferred an in-person visit to Grand Rapids, I had a wonderful time meeting and talking with students, faculty, staff, and members the community. GRCC is a most relevant and responsive shining star of the community college movement. It is a college on a journey with no end, working to create a world that could be. GRCC is a genuine anchor of community. This is what democracy looks like.

Reflections

Grand Rapids, Michigan, was ranked 13th in the country by *U.S. News and World Report* as one of the best places to live in America, but not for everyone. In fact, *Forbes* magazine (Kotkin, 2015) ranked the city as one of the worst cities in America for African Americans. Since being ranked 51st out of 52 cities that were doing the worst economically for Black Americans, Grand Rapids has engaged in a citywide effort to address systemic racism. The work at GRCC is an instrumental part of this effort. Under the leadership of President Pink, the college community recognizes the need to "widen the circle" of prosperity, opportunity, and outcomes. Thus, as President

Pink described, the institution has been deepening their commitment to being "relevant and responsive to [their selves], [their] students, and [their] community" through a broad equity agenda.

The COVID-19 health pandemic and the ongoing racial pandemic forced GRCC to rethink what it means to be relevant and responsive. A study by the Hope Center for College, Community, and Justice (Goldrick-Rab et al., 2020) found that nearly half of all GRCC students experienced moderate to severe anxiety and 32% were taking care of at least one family member as a result of COVID-19. Thirty-five percent of students who were working before the health crisis lost their jobs, while another 30% had their hours and/or pay reduced. These and other issues leave students with little time or energy to focus on learning, transfer, and/or degree completion.

While COVID-19 continues to wreak havoc in our country and around the world at the time of this writing, the impact of the health pandemic was minimized at GRCC due to what Sophia Brewer, serials and collections development librarian, observed as "effective leadership, a focus on student success and demonstrated care for employees" (Grand Rapids Community College TV [GRCCtv], 2020, 5:27). GRCC expanded its food pantry, waived all fees for summer classes, and donated PPE to local hospitals. In addition, they've developed a loaner laptop program complete with hotspots, web cameras, and free technology support 7 days week. They also partnered with the Kent District Library to increase Wi-Fi access for GRCC students throughout the region.

While the entire campus appeared to be engaged in GRCC's equity agenda, a great deal of credit is attributed to McNeely Cobham. As the college's inaugural chief equity and inclusion officer, she is charged with helping the institution meet its strategic equity goals around eliminating disparities in educational access, student success, faculty and staff development, and community partnerships. Specifically, one of the college's core goals in the 3-year strategic plan is equity, including three college action projects (CAPs): (a) close achievement gaps for targeted groups; (b) build an inclusive campus for all; and (c) establish a single-stop center that connects GRCC students to food, housing, and emergency cash. To succeed in these efforts, McNeely Cobham said she and her team provide the campus community "support and advocacy, assessment and strategic planning, recruitment and retention, and training and development" (GRCC, 2018, para. 8).

In GRCC's 2020 Equity Report video (GRCCtv, 2020), McNeely Cobham explains that being relevant and responsive "wasn't merely a statement. It was a charge" (00:48). This important rethinking means that she, along with everyone on campus, would need to "be attentive, have empathy, serve above and beyond, act with urgency and justice, have courage, and boldly think outside the box" (GRCCtv, 2020, 00:52). Lina Blair, director of student life and conduct, explained that being relevant and responsive also means that faculty and staff have to intently listen to students and to understand their experiences. To do so, faculty and staff will need to "remove the blinders and their own lived experiences from the equation," a practice that often makes people uncomfortable (1:28).

Sophia Brewer and Mansfield Matheson, director of purchasing, lead the college action project to create a more inclusive campus. I must admit this is one of few times in my higher education career hearing that two people outside of student affairs or the equity office were taking the lead on such work, which suggests depth in the work GRCC is doing. In their CAP leadership roles, they coordinated intergroup dialogue training sessions for faculty and staff, oversaw several equity-centered subcommittees, and held "courageous conversations" with students. Following the social unrest after the killing of George Floyd, the GRCC community has been more reflective of the reach and impact of equity goals. Brewer used campus climate as an example of this reflection, noting that a sense of belonging is beyond the physical space; it is also conscious, requiring GRCC faculty and staff to rethink what an inclusive campus looks like in a remote environment.

In addition to town hall discussions and courageous conversations, the Office of Diversity, Equity, and Inclusion held space for students, faculty, and staff to talk about the 2020 presidential election, before, during, and after November 3rd. While we did not talk to McNeely Cobham after the election, Michigan was the center of much attention throughout the election cycle. Given the size and diversity of the college and state, not to mention the dramatic certification of 2020 election results in Michigan, these discussions must have been important to the community and must not have been easy.

The work that GRCC is engaged in regarding being relevant and responsive through an equity lens is challenging and ongoing. President Pink is quick to remind you that they are still on their journey and the journey itself is what matters. As both President Pink and Professor McNeely Cobham emphasized, the road ahead is a windy one, as not everyone within the college community are prepared for the changes that must come if they are to reach their goals and continue to amplify opportunity for a more racially and ethnically diverse community.

Often when one talks about systemic racism within an institution, college community members may be concerned about the negative connotation that it places on the institution and themselves. The work that GRCC is doing, however, places the college on a path to address and remove factors that perpetuate systemic racism that is embedded into the fabric of American society, including higher education (Harper et al., 2009). The equity work that McNeely Cobham is leading at GRCC is also instrumental in the college achieving its economic and educational goals. As Reverend Jones noted, "GRCC is an on-ramp for economic mobility, and they are committed to widening the circle of opportunity."

The Promise Zone Scholarship is an example of the ways GRCC's work in equity supports widening educational opportunities, in this case for high school students in the city of Grand Rapids. At first glance the Promise Zone Scholarship resembles that of other states' merit scholarship programs that became popular in the mid-1990s to help keep state residents in the state. While Michigan does have such a merit scholarship, it is not the Promise Zone award. In fact, there are not requirements for grade point average (GPA) or other academic criteria. Attending high school within the city is the primary eligibility criterion. As the GRCC (n.d.) website explains, "All students should be given the opportunity to continue their education" (para. 15).

This is increasingly important as local companies rely on GRCC to provide them with educated and trained employees. GRCC's America's Promise Grant helps the college fulfill this need. Since 2016, GRCC has worked with more than 12 organizations within the region to provide more than 1,500 people career coaching and tuition assistance. More than 1,000 people enrolled in health-care training programs. Job placement is at 94% (GRCC, 2019). As employers are looking for well-trained employees, the equity work GRCC is engaged in ensures companies will also have access to socially just employees as well.

Discussion Questions

1. What is the role of a chief diversity officer? In what ways can or should college presidents support the work of a chief diversity officer?
2. In what ways is systemic racism embedded in higher education? How does it show up within community colleges? What responsibility do community college administrators have to address it in their institutions and in their communities?
3. In what ways can an institutional leader engage an entire campus in addressing short- and long-term community needs?
4. What does it mean for an institution to be relevant and responsive? Why is it important for community colleges to be relevant and responsive to the needs of their community?

8

DINÉ COLLEGE

My grandchild, education is the ladder. Tell our people to take it.

—Chief, Hastinn Ch'il Haajiin (Manuelito; 1893, para. 2)

I t did not take long into the conversation with President Charles M. Roessel (Monty) to understand that Diné College is a college of, by, and for the people of the Navajo Nation (*Naabeehó Bináhásdzo*). President Roessel was clearly proud, yet humble, when talking about the Diné mission, philosophy, and impact of the college.

"Everything on this earth is interconnected and related," President Roessel said. He went on, "What happens way over there impacts what happens right here. It's the philosophy of the college: *Sa'ah Naaghái Bik'eh Hózhóón*. What it means is about where we fit in nature, where nature fits in us, where we fit in the world, where the world fits us, how we're in balance and harmony, and that our goal is to reach that balance and harmony. And sometimes it's out of balance, and our philosophy of education is: How do you get back in balance?"

Diné is a very personal and familial experience for all the students, faculty, and staff I talked with, none more so than President Roessel. That is in part because Robert Roessel, Monty's father, was the first president of Navajo Community College. He was among the first to call for the creation of a Navajo Department of Education, which was established in 2005.

When talking about Robert Roessel, Navajo Nation President Joe Shirley Jr. said, "Our Navajo family has truly lost one of our sons, one of our brothers." He added,

> Dr. Roessel came to our land as a young man and embraced our culture with his whole heart. Then he taught us, one after another, to love who we are as individuals, as a people and as a culture. The meaning of his life was to teach the Navajo people to love the wisdom and teachings of our

medicine people and to combine that with the highest attainment of academic achievement so that we could live in true sovereignty as individuals and as a nation. He took immense pride when his own Navajo students went on to achieve a college degree. He will be deeply missed. (Hardeen, 2006, para. 3)

According to many at Diné College, President Robert Roessel mentored thousands of Navajo students, as well as staff who worked under him, about the importance of knowing their grandparents' teachings, using the Navajo language, and living the Navajo culture in their daily lives. Monty added, "Dad was a leader of heart and mind; the universities filled his mind, but it was my mom that taught him the way of the heart, the Navajo way."

Monty talked about how he has followed in his dad's footsteps, "first at Rough Rock and then here at Diné College. . . . It is an honor to be here; it is a calling to serve a mission, not just the college mission, something larger, it is to serve the Nation . . . to honor the elders as my dad did." He then started to talk about serving the students at Diné College. As he was talking, he had to stop; his eyes filled. His pause was filled with the honest emotion of understanding, compassion, and respect for Diné students' journeys. "It is such an honor to serve these students. . . to tell the stories of Diné College is to tell the stories of Navajo Nation."

Monty once asked his dad, "How did you get into education and become an educator?" His dad replied, "I am not an educator, I am a community developer, and I do that work through education." Monty added, "That tells you a lot about Diné College as well as my dad." He went on, "Dad was pretty big at the time, teaching at the university. I loved living in Tempe; it was so much fun running around the neighborhood. . . . Then one day Dad said we were moving here to the Nation, adding 'You can sit around and talk, or you can do.'"

"There is one story that is most significant to Diné College," said Monty on our Zoom call. "Raymond Nakai, then chairman of the Navajo Nation, and Dad were friends. They would often talk and think big thoughts about education, community, and the Nation. . . . One day they said, 'enough is enough.'" Monty interjected, "Just like the response to George Floyd, enough is enough. . . . My Dad and Raymond said it is time to create a college by Navajo people for Navajo people. It is time for us to control our own education."

The Navajo Nation is an American Indian territory covering 27,413 square miles in northeastern Arizona, southeastern Utah, and northwestern New Mexico. It is the largest land area retained by an Indigenous tribe in the United States.

Over 150 public, private, and Bureau of Indian Affairs schools serve Navajo students from kindergarten through high school. Most schools are funded from the Navajo Nation under the federally funded Johnson O'Malley program. The Nation runs community Head Start programs, the only educational program fully operated by the Navajo Nation government. Postsecondary education and vocational training are available on and off the territory.

Navajo Community College was established by the people of Navajo Nation to serve the people of Navajo Nation in 1968 "to encourage Navajo youth to become contributing members of the Navajo Nation and the world society" (Diné College, 2020b, para. 1). In 1997 the college changed its name to Diné College. The word *diné* in the Navajo language means "people." Diné College was the first college established by Native Americans for Native Americans. Since then, 32 tribal colleges have been established on numerous reservations.

The main campus of Diné College is in Tsaile, Arizona. Other locations include Chinle, Crownpoint, Shiprock, Tuba City, and Window Rock. Diné offers 12 Bachelor of Science degrees, 20 Associate of Art degrees, and nine certificate programs. Fall 2020 student enrollment was 1,300 compared to 1,463 for the fall of 2019. Given the pandemic's impact, the 2020 enrollment far exceeded projections.

According to the Diné website, the 2018 annual report, and 2019 IPEDS data, 65% of Diné 1st-year students report as female, 35% male; 45% attended full-time, and 55% attended part-time. Students ranged in age from 18–64, with the vast majority between the ages of 25 and 34. The full-time cost (tuition, fees, room and board) is $6,350. The graduation rate is 17%, retention rate 46%, and transfer-out rate 35%. Ninety-eight percent of the students report as American Indian or Alaska Native; 2% report as non-American Indian or Alaska Native. There are 68 full-time faculty and 237 full-time employees, of which 68% identify as Navajo (Diné College, 2021).

Diné College awards bachelor and associate degrees and certificates in areas important to the economic and social development of the Navajo Nation. In 1998, it bestowed its first baccalaureate degrees under the Diné Teacher Education program, accredited under a partnership with Arizona State University.

To answer the question of whether Diné College enhances upward social mobility, a core tenet of the American Dream, I thought it was essential to understand the definition of social mobility for the Navajo people. It differs from that of Western society. In the West, social mobility is often defined as the degree to which people within a society move up or down a class system, for the most part defined by one's income, occupation, or status. In *The Navajo Reservation, the Navajo People, and Social Mobility*, Davina Two Bears (2014) writes about the Navajo definition of social mobility:

> Navajo people regard having a family and maintaining positive interaction with one's family, which may include the extended family and clan relatives, as an indicator of high status. If a Navajo person were to find themselves without family, they may experience a downward social mobility in Navajo society. For many Navajo people, achieving success includes maintaining hózhó, harmony in one's life, by practicing good health and wellness—mentally, physically, and spiritually. One of the most important indications of "wealth" in Navajo society is the existence of family, which includes those related biologically and through the clans. Having a family and maintaining healthy relationships with one's extended family and clan relatives is highly regarded in Navajo society. In Navajo society, maintaining one's culture/language; positive relationships with one's natal, extended and clan families; and demonstrating K'e defines an upward social mobility. In Western society, the accumulation of financial wealth is an indication of upward social mobility, but in Navajo society, "wealth" goes beyond money and includes having family and demonstrating K'e, even if you are not financially well off. (p. 1)

The Navajo people are a matrilineal/matriarchal society, where clan membership is passed through the women, and women are highly respected. Every Navajo has four clans: the mother's clan (the main clan), father's clan, maternal grandfather's clan, and paternal grandfather's clan.

As the Zoom meetings unfolded and the introductions began, I learned that it is customary to first share the identity of one's clan to determine the relatedness among Navajo people. That is how people introduced themselves to me and each other in all my Zoom calls, especially so college students.

The extraordinary journeys of the Diné College students I met filled and moved me. For Diné students, a commitment to create a better life for themselves and family also requires a commitment to create a better life for all in the Navajo Nation. One of the students expressed it this way: "They taught me that it is my responsibility, it is what we learn from birth, it is woven into everything we learn here. . . . All Diné students, all faculty and staff, all in Navajo Nation are my family. . . . I feel a profound connection and commitment to my sisters, my brothers, my grandparents and my parents, it is the way of "K'e."

Professor Smith, an alum, who was the Diné College comptroller before earning her doctorate and moving into the faculty ranks said, "I see myself in my students, and my hope is that students can see themselves in me."

Educators around the world understand the power of belonging and community in teaching and learning. The most successful teachers and leaders know how to create the environments that create those relationships for students. The learning outcomes are powerful, empowering, and sustaining. That is what *K'e* means to the Navajo Nation, and that is also what it means to the students, faculty, and staff at Diné College.

President Monty Roessel also talked about *K'e* in our initial conversation. "It means relationship, the kind of relationship we all have with each other in a community. It speaks to the responsibility we have to one another. K'e is part of who we are at Diné; it is part of our core." I learned about Diné's educational philosophy, *Sa'ah Naaghái Bik'eh Hózhóón* and *K'e*, all throughout my visit.

K'e is a Navajo word that describes the maintenance of positive, loving, and healthy family relationships. Each of the students, faculty, and staff I met described the Diné experience as a feeling of "belonging, family, and home," many telling me, "It starts as a child . . . as a Navajo."

The culture of Navajo Nation is significant to the culture at Diné College. "The responsibility we have to others, that feeling of family and home, is written into our core values as a college," said Crystal Cree, director of legislative affairs and policy, pointing to the college's document hanging on the wall of her office.

A Diné student told me, "I grew up feeling that education took something from me. I was bullied as a child in school because I only spoke Navajo. . . . After high school I stayed with my grandmother to take care of her. I never even thought of college. After she passed, I had a child. . . . My husband and I were living in a car. . . . I remember driving passed a billboard that said, 'Start your future at Diné.' So, we came just to see what it was like here. . . . Diné literally saved my life. The people here are my family. I no longer feel that education takes something from you. Every day I feel just how much Diné has given me."

Yet another student added, "I started at [university], but I left because I felt something was missing. I didn't know what it was, but I knew something was missing. So, I came home. My mother said that I should come here to Diné just to see what they had to offer until I knew what university I wanted to go to. I now know what it was that was missing . . . K'e, that feeling that I am part of a family, that I have all of my sisters and brothers watching out for me, just as I watch out for them. I belong here at Diné . . . and when I get my graduate degree, doing research, I will carry that with me. . . . I now know that I am never alone."

One student, who arrived late because he was interviewing for an internship said, "When I enter a room and see my sisters, or in this case see their names on the screen, I have to sit up straight, pay attention, and do my best. That is what they expect from me." He added, "I went to Navajo Prep School in Farmington [New Mexico] and was honored to graduate with a Navajo Nation scholarship. My classmates went to schools like Harvard, MIT, Berkeley, University of Arizona, or ASU [Arizona State University]. I could have attended any one of those colleges, but I wanted to come here to Diné College. . . . I wanted to learn more about the teachings of the Navajo Nation. I hope to continue my learning about the ways of my elders, especially about government and leadership. I want to become a Navajo scholar."

More than one of the students I met with talked about the intersectionality of Navajo and Western knowledge at Diné: "I learn philosophy, history, and the Navajo way in every class I take. Even in my biology classes. . . . I learn the Western ways of science, but I also learn about my history; I learn life lessons and about the culture of my people. I learn more about me and my connection to my family, my people in every class I take. . . . I did not appreciate who I was until I came here to Diné." Another added, "Everyone here teaches us about the connections between all things. . . . I think Western science is understanding how everything is connected, more and more."

One student reflected on what she had learned from the Diné president. "Dr. Roessel often talks about the importance of giving back, of paying it forward, of taking care of others. I think that is how we make our community and our families stronger." Another said, "My getting an education teaches my children about the importance of education. They see me studying and working hard; I believe they will do the same."

I thought about that last comment and what that same student had said earlier about how education "took things" from her. In just one generation, a student has changed from a feeling that education takes something away from you to one that understands how education adds to her life and that it will benefit her children. Talk about profound impact and moving needles.

Whether they live in Greenfield, Massachusetts; Warner, Oklahoma; South Bronx, NYC; Grand Rapids, Michigan; or the Navajo Nation, even after 40 years of service, the lives, aspirations, and determination of community college students to create a better life for themselves and their families continues to inspire me. Their day-to-day struggle against the oppressive forces of poverty, racism, classism, and sexism is nothing short of heroic. Community college students deserve better from our nation. It is in America's best interest to do so.

The harmony and interconnectedness that is part of the Diné philosophy is also found in the design of the campus. Of all the college campuses I have visited over the course of my career, albeit this time virtually, I thought the interconnecting circles within circles design of Diné was among the most interesting. It is built in the traditions of the Navajo culture. Students, faculty, and staff talked about the campus as "home" and a feeling of "harmony."

Vice President Glennita Haskey said, "When you go away and come back, there is a sacred sense, a feeling of direction. You know that the Ned Hatatchle Cultural Center (NHC) is at the east entrance and that is where all of your thought process is. . . . Classrooms are sitting on the south side, where knowledge happens . . . [the] west side is where the dorms are, the Hogans (sacred homes for the Navajo people), the place to rest, revive, and collect yourself. . . . On the north side is the gym for leisure and life activities. You enter the circle of the campus, and you just have the feeling I am home. I know that regardless of my uniqueness and my challenges there is a place for me here. I'm home and I know how to conduct myself. . . . Everywhere you go you treat people as family. . . . That is how you are in harmony at Diné."

Provost Geraldine Garrity, Professor Miranda Haskie, and Professor Perry H. Charley talked about the significant ways in which the Diné educational philosophy is a true north navigational tool. Found on their website, Diné College's educational philosophy "places Diné life in harmony with the natural world and the universe. Grounded in Navajo cultural traditions, the philosophy provides principles for protection from the imperfections in life and for the development of well-being" (Diné College, 2020a, paras. 1–2).

According to the Diné website, the core of this philosophy is expressed in concepts and values associated with natural processes identified with "the four cardinal directions, including such processes as the daily cycle of day and night and the annual cycle of the seasons" (Diné College, 2020a, para. 1). Diné College fulfills its mission by using the *Sa'ah Naaghái Bik'eh Hozhoo* principle as a framework to educate its students:

- "*Nitsáhákees* (thinking), *Nahat'á* (planning), *Iiná* (living), and *Sihasin* (assuring)
- studying Diné language, history, and culture
- preparing for further studies and employment in a multicultural and technological world
- fostering social responsibility, community service, and scholarly research that contribute to the social, economic, and cultural well-being of the Navajo Nation" (Diné College, 2018, p. 2)

Professor Charley told me about why he came to Diné after working as a nuclear researcher for the government: "Over the years, many researchers have come to our community wanting to learn more about the Navajo. They study us and then leave. They never come back and help us fix the problems that they are researching. I wanted to teach our people how to do that research for themselves. Our people will stay in our community and will use those tools to address our problems. That is why I am here. That is the privilege of teaching science here at Diné."

I told Perry that just the day before one of his students asked me, "Before I begin to tell you my story, can you talk about reciprocity, what you are willing to give back from your research?" Professor Charley didn't say a word, but I could see pride in his eyes. I added, "It is education by us and for us." Garrity and Haskie just smiled, as if to say, "I think he gets it."

I asked Professor Haskie to say more about the ways in which Diné teachers are able to integrate language, culture, and history into every content class. She said, "By teaching language, culture, and history in every class and requiring it as part of our core, we want our students to have a deeper understanding of who they are and where they came from." Provost Garrity talked about how Diné, through its many partnerships and institutes, has become a significant resource for government, education, business, and the arts. Each in their own voice and in their own words added that it is a way of empowering each student and sustaining Navajo Nation.

Examples of that "by us, for us" research and examples of the community resources Diné College provides include a summer research project on the impact of COVID-19 in Navajo Nation, the Diné Policy Institute, the Diné Language Immersion Institute, and the Diné Environmental Institute. Because of the work of students and Professor Haskie, Diné College is also the largest repository of "living oral history" of the Navajo Nation. According to Professor Haskie, "Our students have captured Navajo living histories that include prominent educators, artists, and leaders on the Navajo Nation, long-time Diné College and Navajo Community College employees, and the world renowned Navajo code talkers."

As the meeting with Provost Garrity, Professor Charley, and Professor Haskie was ending, I waved and said goodbye. Provost Garrity interjected, saying that there is no word for goodbye in the Navajo language. Instead, she shared with me the Navajo word *hagoonee.* Perry added, "It means we will pick up where we left off next time we meet."

No college in America has been more negatively impacted by the pandemic of 2020 than Diné. The impact from COVID-19 at the college and the Navajo Nation has been acute, critical, and deadly. According to President Monty Roessel, "The need is so great at Diné we don't even know the totality of the need. You're not going to make any great changes if you're just working around the edges." He added, "We need to redefine what equity means in Indian country." He told us that 30% of the people in the Navajo Nation do not have running water, and only 8.3% have some postsecondary education (Ashford, 2020, paras. 7–8).

In my first conversation with the president, he said that a majority of students indicated last spring that they don't want to come back in person this coming fall, and now most prefer online classes. Health and safety are critical for a college where the average age of faculty is 65.

According to the AACC, 95.4% of full-time community college students live at home and commute. The average distance traveled to school by community college students is about 10 miles one way. President Roessel told me that students at Diné are traveling 60 or 100 miles to campus. "It doesn't make sense to come for one class."

He also talked about the lack of broadband as a major problem for Diné students. "We have students who have to hike half a mile up a hill just to get a signal to take a class." President Roessel directed staff to drive around and check how many bars they had on their phones at different locations. "We have to start looking at education without boundaries," he said. He is planning to create learning centers in different areas of the reservation that K–12 and university students can use, as well as students at the community college.

Diné College provided $700 to full-time students and $475 to part-time students through its allotment from the CARES Act. The college used other funds for the 200 students who didn't qualify for CARES money. One challenge at Diné is that many students don't have bank accounts. So instead of direct deposit, students waited in their cars for hours in long lines to pick up their checks. And for those who could not get to the campus, faculty and staff delivered the checks to their houses. President Roessel wants to convince Congress to provide the $2 million a year for operations and maintenance that was promised but not funded. The Navajo Nation, 27,000 square miles across the states of Arizona, New Mexico, and Utah, has had the largest per-capita infection rate in the nation.

Each of the faculty and staff I talked with told me some of the many stories of those impacted by the pandemic. Professor Smith's comment struck a chord: "I would call or write to my students, and although I never wanted them to have to relive their trauma, I would ask, 'How are you?'"

Crystal and Velveena said, "We don't have the technology for direct deposits yet, and some of our students couldn't get here, so we drove to our students' homes to deliver those CARES checks." They went on to talk about the many 2-hour drives to the nearest grocery stores that might still have some food on the shelf, after a day working at the college, trying to get home before the curfew imposed by the president of Navajo Nation.

In part because of the matriarchal culture of Navajo Nation, much of the housing is multigenerational. The virus took its toll on those families and households. Many talked about their students and their own families who had died or fallen sick. Haskey told me, "I was scared for my family, all of my family, but as a woman leader, I did not have the privilege of showing any fear. As a Navajo woman, I am a leader, a warrior for my people, especially here at Diné. . . . I would meditate and pray. I prayed hard for my family at home and my family here at the college." She added, "There were many good outcomes here at Diné during that period, in part because we could not be with our families, like when my mother was in the hospital . . . so we came here—it is also a home for us; these people are my family."

I have learned a great deal about Diné as a college, as a nation, and as a way of life during my time visiting with students, faculty, and staff. Diné College is unique, shaped and framed by the community it serves, the Navajo Nation. Founded on an empowering vision of "by us, for us," it is clear to me that Diné is an anchor of and for the Navajo people, the community's college making good on the mandates of its mission: "Rooted in Diné language and culture, our mission is to advance quality post-secondary student learning and development to ensure the well-being of the Diné People" (Diné College, 2020b, para. 5). Diné's 5,571 alumni are the teachers, nurses, researchers, artists, Navajo scholars, and government leaders who are strengthening family, community, and nations.

At some point in one of our conversations President Roessel said to me, "Dad loved all sports but especially baseball. He came to every event for all of his kids, but he loved baseball the most. You knew you did well if he said, 'You played with courage,' not great hit or wonderful play or nice win. . . . You played with courage was the best compliment Dad could give you." It was clear to me in all my visits that the students, faculty, staff, and leadership of Diné College are teaching, learning, and leading with courage.

My visit was all too brief. I left Diné before I wanted to. There was a warmth of spirit, a harmony, and a sense of balance there that was familiar yet all too distant. Each of the good people I talked with had given me a most wonderful present. They didn't just talk about Diné College and the Navajo Nation with me, they welcomed me into it. And given that they are now my sisters and brothers, I have a responsibility to them, to give back to them all that they had given to me. It is the way of *K'e*. Hagoonee.

Reflections

As we have discussed in previous chapters, community colleges, whether located in rural or urban contexts, play a vital role in their communities. This is especially true when that community college is a tribal college. Tribal colleges and universities (TCUs) are two- or four-year institutions that serve predominantly Native students and have a majority of Native Americans on their governing boards (American Indian College Fund, 2011). TCUs, in themselves, are institutions built with the community (i.e., Indigenous people) at the forefront. In fact, Tribal Colleges are designed with the intention of nation building and the preservation of language and culture.

As Bob rightfully noted in this chapter, Robert Roessel was the first president of Diné College and was a founder of the school. Roessel, however, was not alone in this important achievement. Current President Monty Roessel spoke about the important role his mother played in Diné's founding. Ruth Roessel always maintained a vision for bringing community-controlled education to the reservation. Having experienced the trauma of U.S. government boarding schools where she was taught that Navajo culture had no value if she was to "assimilate" to white society, Ruth knew how incredibly important it is for the Diné people to understand the value of a Navajo education. As her daughter, Faith, recalled about her mother's belief and understanding, "If our children are proud of who they are, if they know who they are, they are going to be successful" (Billy, 2019, para. 5).

After returning to the reservation from ASU, the Roessels sought to create Rough Rock Demonstration School, a teaching training school, for the Diné people. In a 2018 interview, Ruth Roessel explained:

> My original goal was I wanted the Navajo kids to remain Navajo, and keep their language and keep their culture and keep the values that makes us Navajo. So, because I've been off-reservation when I went to school and all this stuff, I learned that it wasn't right. I looked at myself as I learned both sides, the cultures and then speaking both languages. So I thought to myself that the little kids at Rough Rock should be learning the [Navajo] language, and English, and to read and write. And so I wanted them to do it—that was my goal. (Haskie & Shreve, 2018, para. 11)

Rough Rock Demonstration School, now Rough Rock Community School, was such a success that people from all over the United States and the world came to observe not only how Navajo language, culture, and history were embedded into the curriculum but also how the local community was involved in the school's governance.

Instead of returning to ASU, the Roessels stayed on the reservation. They, along with Raymond Nakai, then chairman of Navajo Nation and a long-time friend of the Roessels, worked to develop a college on the reservation, in part to address high levels of students dropping out from non-Native colleges and universities. Soon thereafter, with the approval of the Navajo Tribal Council, Navajo Community College, now Diné College, was born. Ruth went on to become the director of Navajo Studies [name of the dept] and helped other universities develop Indigenous studies programs. She also documented first-person accounts of Navajo history in two edited publications of Navajo Community College.

Ruth talked about the way Navajo students, who went on to study across the United States, returned to Diné College because they wanted to learn their culture and language, to "learn about who they are" (Haskie & Shreve, 2018, para. 21). The importance of students learning and in some cases remembering what it means to be Diné is an important characteristic that has remained since the day Diné College first opened its doors in 1968, as the first tribally controlled institution in the United States.

We have often, in this book, talked about institutions' maintaining ownership of their activities and being accountable to the communities they serve. We talked about the importance of institutions demonstrating a mantra of "for us, by us." Diné College deepens the meaning of that phrase as their mission is to develop Navajo students and graduates to be contributing members of the Navajo Nation and beyond. In other words, as President Monty Roessel stated, Diné College is a "higher education institution of the Navajo people, for the Navajo people, by Navajo people" (Bennett-Begaye, 2018, para. 8).

It was therefore important for the college to be governed by Navajo people. Diné College is governed by a board of regents, appointed by the president of Navajo Nation. Perhaps more than any other institution we visited in this book, Diné College, in its policies, practices, and community, also demonstrates that "nothing about us, without us, is for us." One of my students, Cynthia Orellana, reminded me of this important phrase from the South African disability rights movement of the 1980s. It offers a deeper understanding of "for us, by us" and Diné College, because in this case it demands that no policy or practice should be implemented without the full participation and support of the Diné people. Thus, the college's strategic goals revolve around preserving the language, history, and culture of the Navajo through formal academic and support programs. Their educational programs are designed to cultivate Nation building to put the Navajo Nation (as opposed to just the institution) in a better economic position. While students talked about learning Western education alongside the ways of the Navajo, the college is designed for self-determination not assimilation. As Bob indicated, "To tell the stories of Diné College is to tell the stories of Navajo Nation." The institution is the Nation, and the Nation is the college.

Sense of Belonging

The students Bob talked to shared how they felt at home at Diné College and had a great sense of belonging. This sense of belonging is particularly important as it is the foundation of persistence. Indeed, at non-Native colleges and universities, many Native students find themselves isolated, separated from family, and subject to negative racial interactions (Tachine et al., 2017). This is why Diné's focus on *K'e* is so important to student success.

Students and President Monty Roessel talked about relationships with each other and the relationship they have with the larger community, a relationship that also carries responsibility. Given the painful and traumatic history tribal communities have had with Western education, these relationships, as core values of the institution, are a critical part of student success. Imagine if all colleges and universities exhibited a responsibility to cultivate relationships between not only faculty, staff, and students but also families and communities. I imagine that more students would enroll, engage in, and complete higher education if more institutions instilled a sense of *K'e*.

While there is much to celebrate in terms of culture and history, present-day challenges and vestiges of the past continue to haunt tribal communities and colleges. While enrollment in tribal colleges has increased, Native student enrollment in both undergraduate and post-baccalaureate Native and non-Native institutions has decreased since 2010 (Marroquín, 2019; Postsecondary National Policy Institute [PNPI], 2020). Moreover, only 25% of Native adults over 25 years old held an associate degree or higher, compared to 42% of all Americans (PNPI, 2020).

Many of the current educational outcomes and social challenges facing Diné people, as well as most Native American tribes, can be directly linked to the U.S. government-controlled boarding schools designed to force Native people to assimilate to European American culture and academics. While it is evident that family and relationships are critical to Navajo people, the U.S. government, from 1860 to 1978, forced hundreds of thousands of Diné and other Native children to travel sometimes thousands of miles from their homes and away from their families. As Ruth Roessel experienced, children were forced to learn English and forbidden to speak their native language. As a result, many Native American tribes lost their languages. Some families, scarred by their own experiences in the so-called boarding schools, will not even teach their own children the Navajo (Diné) language at home out of fear that their children will suffer the same trauma they did (Arviso, 2020).

Exploring the scope and depth of horror found in these federally controlled boarding schools is beyond the scope of this chapter or book; however, it is important to acknowledge this history as it helps to explain why and how the work of Diné College is so critically important. It is not surprising then, that current President Roessel talked about the need to "get back in balance." Indeed, without Diné College, the Navajo language, culture, and history may have otherwise been lost. As Arviso (2020) points out, these "classes have afforded a revitalization of their local tribal customs" (p. 78).

Further, while the college and Navajo Nation continue to face challenges, there has been a 19% rise in adults between the ages of 25 and 29 who hold an associate degree between 2010 and 2019.

At Diné College, while enrollment was down in fall 2020 due to COVID-19, it was still higher than expected. Diné College continues to play a vital role in, with, and for the community. In December 2019, legal scholars from across the United States gathered at Diné College to discuss plans for a law school, a long-time goal of the college. If they are successful, it will be the first tribally controlled law school, demonstrating again how Diné is leading the way in tribal education.

Discussion Questions

1. What does it mean to "teach and lead with courage"?
2. How important is it for a community college to be culturally relevant? What does that mean to you?
3. In what ways should all community colleges create a sense of belonging for all students? In what ways do community colleges you are familiar with develop relationships between students, their families, and the college faculty and staff?
4. What role do higher education and community colleges play in supporting, valuing, and celebrating communities' history, culture, and language?
5. What lessons does Diné College, particularly its commitment to the Navajo Nation, have for other community colleges that are not Tribal Colleges?

9

BERKELEY CITY COLLEGE

The gem cannot be polished without friction, nor man perfected without trials.

—Chinese Proverb

"There is no footprint for new presidents during a pandemic," Angélica Garcia said during our first meeting. Just to be sure, I looked up "pandemics and first presidencies" in all the leadership books I have. Nope, I couldn't find any "how-to" manuals. Garcia is trailblazing. She is among a small cohort who have accepted a leadership position in higher education, just as COVID-19 was shutting down campuses across America.

"I haven't been able to interact in-person with many colleagues. . . . There are no informal opportunities to build relationships, like stopping by an office or passing in the hallways. . . . It just isn't an option." Garcia added, "It's a challenge for sure, though not one that's insurmountable. I have felt nothing but love and a warm welcome in all the virtual phone and videoconferencing spaces that we have." Garcia was appointed president of Berkeley City College in Berkeley, California, May 7, 2020. Berkeley City College is one of the colleges in the Peralta Community College District.

As President Garcia walked into the virtual president's office at Berkeley City College, she embraced the challenge. "It is humbling to understand all that there is to know in this position. . . . I knew I had a lot to learn." She added, "It is important to me as a leader to be transparent about the fact that I don't know everything there is to know." It was also important to her that she reach out as soon as possible to all her new colleagues. "They were all so gracious and welcoming to me," President Garcia said, adding, "for all of the loss of not being able to meet with people in person, people in the community have been most receptive to meeting with me remotely. . . . Old-fashioned phone calls work well."

At the same time, President Garcia has been fortified by a community of scholars and long-time friends. "I have the same colleagues and friends

146

that I have worked with and learned with over the course of my career, [and] most of them came before all the titles and degrees. . . . I still talk with them on a regular basis." She added, "These critical colleagues were integral in the diversity, equity, and inclusion work I have done throughout my career."

I don't know of a successful president in higher education who does not have that small and trusted group or person that they can rely on and learn with. Walking into a presidency without that kind of support would be difficult, and I imagine that it would be almost impossible to do so during this pandemic.

President Garcia identifies as a "first-generation student and a first generation professional." She shared with me her experience transitioning from theory to application: "It is hard to explain, but I feel at a very deep level that I now own this. . . . I truly and deeply understand my responsibilities to the students, faculty, staff and this community."

Talking about the current environment at Berkeley City College, President Garcia said, "People are emotionally taxed right now . . . and that is not unique to our college; I think that is true in all of higher education." The president said it was therefore important for her to model healthy behavior. "I want to model balance. . . . I try to only work one night a week now. . . . Like many of my colleagues, I am balancing working, supporting my children through their online learning [kindergarten and fifth grade], and trying to stay balanced."

At the same time, President Garcia looks at every invitation as "an opportunity to establish relationships and build community. . . . So whether it is a Friday night or on a weekend, I am there. . . . The truth is that I have fallen in love with this college . . . the people, the building, our history . . . and I'm really excited about our future."

COVID-19 is only one of the challenges that President Garcia, faculty, and staff of Berkeley City College have to face. The brutal killing of George Floyd, Breonna Taylor, and Ahmaud Arbery and the shooting of Jacob Blake all became part of a rallying cry in cities and towns across the country, forcing the United States to confront the racism of its past and present. The summer of 2020 became one of racial reckoning.

Kuni Hay, vice president of instruction, talked about how her own journey with racism and growing up in Hawaii impacted her commitment to community college students and her current leadership position. "I wanted this position of power for students. . . . I wanted to have impact on the decisions that impact their lives." Hay added emphatically, "We are definitely making a commitment to our antiracism work here, in and out of our classrooms."

Martin De Mucha Flores, associate dean for educational success, talked about meeting the technology needs of students during the pandemic, and he also talked about how proud he is of the college. "BCC is speaking out about systemic racism. . . . There is great support for Black and Hispanic students here . . . not just in our statements but more important, by our actions."

Both pandemics had to be addressed, and as an anchor institution, Berkeley responded. Leadership, faculty, and staff looked for ways to meet the needs of students—from food, shelter, and technology to the need for community and the emotional well-being of students, faculty, and staff alike.

I asked Stacy Shears, vice president of student services, about Berkeley City College students during the pandemic. "It has been hard on so many of our students. . . . They relied so heavily on our little building. . . . It has also been hard on our local businesses too, in part because we are not here. . . . These are hard times for a lot of people."

"It is important that students, faculty, and staff feel safe here at [Berkeley City College] . . . that we create a climate that is welcoming," said the director of business services, Shirley Slaughter. She then talked about "how important language is" in the creation of that space and place: "For example," she said, "instead of saying 'social distance,' we should instead emphasize physical distance."

Librarian Heather Dodge talked about the partnership with the local food pantry. "It is a partnership that benefits both students and community. Too many students . . . too many in our community, go hungry. That partnership addresses many of those needs."

Many talked about the good work of John Nguyen, campus life director, including the development of the school's food pantry. Nguyen started his career serving community college students as a community college student. "I saw a sign at my college that announced there was an opening in student government, so I looked into it." Looking back, Nguyen talked about how that moment changed his life "because of [his] involvement with student government . . . and because of meeting the person who would become [his] mentor." Nguyen added, "I knew I wanted to work with students who were like me . . . those trying to find identity and purpose." It was clear to me that Nguyen found his purpose and his identity in service to students.

Berkeley City College has also been experiencing the tensions of a history that saw the college transition from adult learning centers, embedded in many quarters of the community, to a comprehensive community college, housed in one building at the center of the city. In recent months, the school was also challenged by the fiscal concerns of the regional accreditation body. With all those changes in space, place, and mission, there were almost as many changes in leadership and governance.

Yet with all those head winds, President Garcia and the college are clearly focused and steely eyed with regard to meeting the mandates of its mission. According to the college's website,

> The Berkeley City College's mission is to provide our diverse community with educational opportunities, and to transform lives. The college achieves its mission through instruction, student support, and learning resources which enable its enrolled students to earn associate degrees and certificates, and to attain college competency, careers, transfer, and skills for lifelong success. (Berkeley City College, 2021, para. 2)

President Garcia told us, "I knew [Berkeley City College] was part of a district that experienced some challenges when I came here, but it is also a district that had shown monumental strides." She added, "[It] has so much social capital, it is such a diamond, a pathway for liberation . . . for all of the issues that face us, Berkeley City College is absolutely an anchor for students, their families, and this community."

The passionate commitment to mission, students, and the community were most apparent in my conversations with faculty and staff. The outcome and impact of that commitment was also apparent in my conversations with students.

Students talked with me about their personal journeys, and they also shared some of the reasons they chose Berkeley City College. Most of those that I talked with mentioned the academic standards, the quality of education, and the transfer rate to UC Berkeley. "I could have gone to another community college closer to my home, but I came here because a friend told me that she got accepted into UC Berkeley because of [Berkeley City College]. That is my goal, and I am confident that [the school] will help me get there."

One of the international students I talked with said, "My father did not want me to attend a college in this country. But when I mentioned Berkeley City College, my dad thought 'Oh Berkeley [thinking university], that's okay.'" The student then added, "I didn't know that [Berkeley City College] transfers so many students to UC Berkeley. I feel like I have a chance to go there now."

Others talked about the importance of affordability alongside the opportunity to take different classes and for exploring majors. "I couldn't afford to go anyplace else. . . . I live pretty close, and so this just made the most sense." Another said, "You could not change courses and you could not change majors in the country where I come from. . . . You take a test and they tell you what classes to take. I changed my major here once already. . . . I understand and appreciate freedom differently now."

Most talked about Berkeley City College as a second chance in education and a second chance at life. One student told me that he was working in the HVAC industry and had "a life-changing illness." He said, "Because of the support of my union, I was able to come here," adding, "this was a second chance at life. . . . I want to learn, and I want to give back." Another said, "I was not prepared as an 18-year-old to go to college and succeed. Today I feel I am."

Felicia Bridges, the school's public information officer, talked about her journey as an example for students. "Like so many of our students here at [Berkeley City College], I wasn't ready for the world. I enrolled at Laney College [one of the colleges in the Peralta Community College System in Oakland], and then went on to UC [Berkeley]." Bridges talked about her experiences as a woman of color, a parent, a wife, and a student—all at the same time. "If I can succeed, anyone can. . . . Life might not be a cakewalk, but if you have faith and the courage to lean on people, and there are so many people here at [Berkeley City College] that you can lean on, then you can achieve your dreams."

Berkeley City College was founded in 1974 as the Berkeley Learning Pavilion, which was renamed the Peralta College for Non-Traditional Study the same year, as a Peralta community college to serve the northern cities of Alameda County: Albany, Berkeley, and Emeryville. The school received initial accreditation through the Accrediting Commission for Community and Junior Colleges (ACCJC) in 1977, and in 1978 it was renamed Vista Community College.

By 1981, the number of locations with classes offered exceeded 200. The same year, it received full accreditation from ACCJC. Between 1994 and 1996, the college attempted to de-annex itself from the Peralta Community College District, but in exchange for dropping the de-annexation effort, the Peralta district built a permanent building for the college in 2006. Before that, classes were offered in many locations throughout the East Bay, including UC Berkeley, West Berkeley YMCA, Berkeley High School, the North Berkeley Community Center, St. Mary Magdalene School, the Summit Educational Center, and the Oakland Army Base. Those that served at those centers remember it fondly.

Professor Marjorie Haskell was sharing a website consisting of political polling data with others when I joined the Zoom call. Professor Haskell teaches political science and has been doing so since 1975. There was no doubt in my conversation with Haskell that she is the holder of the rich history of Berkeley City College. "It felt like a lot of the community folks disappeared when the building was built. . . . We did more lifelong learning back then with older students. . . . We do more transfer work with younger students now."

Professor Haskell's own journey started in Brooklyn, on to Harvard, across America to UC Berkeley, and then she became an elected official in Oakland. Before she left our call for another appointment, she said, "[Berkeley

City College] has always been a doorway to opportunity. . . . That is as true today as it was when I first came here in 1975."

In June 2006, the name of the college was changed to Berkeley City College when it moved into the current building, a six-story, 165,000–square foot campus designed to accommodate approximately 8,000 students. It was built in the heart of the city. On a map, it looks like it is situated in the economic center of Berkeley, directly between Berkeley High School and the university. It seems purposeful, an almost perfect metaphor, and Professor Haskell confirmed that it was intentional. Education and jobs, education and civic engagement, education and economic mobility, education and liberty, education and democracy—one building, so many powerful outcomes.

Growing up in Berkeley and having attended Berkeley High, Andrea Williams, transfer coordinator, said, "I had to leave the community to find out how special this community is . . . and now I get to give back working at this college. . . . It is such an important institution for so many. . . . They wouldn't have access to an education let alone go on to universities like UC Berkeley."

Vice President Shears added, "[The school] is transformative, like we say we are. . . . That happens, in part, because a student can come here and be totally themselves . . . in all of their uniqueness and know that they belong here." Shears said, "[It] is a place for everyone and anyone. . . . It is an educational home for our students."

Lisa Cook, dean of liberal arts, had a big smile on her face on the Zoom screen as I was introducing myself to the administrative leadership team. When she said that she started her career at Mass Bay Community College (in Massachusetts) and was also an alum of UMass Boston, I returned the smile. It's always fun to meet someone from back home when traveling, even when it is virtual.

Cook told me, "As a dean here, I am excited about the work we do with faculty to revise pedagogy. . . . It is important that we live up to our tag line about 'transforming lives.' . . . Empowering students through learning and education is the process for that transformation." She also talked about the college building: "There is high visibility for all at our small campus. . . . You can see and be a part of everything."

Students, faculty, and staff alike talked about the campus building where transparency and community are a way of life and a way of learning. A student I talked with placed a photo of the tutoring center, where he is a tutor, as a backdrop to his Zoom screen. When I asked what the photo was, he told me it was the "Learning Resource Center," adding, "It is such a comfortable space that we all love; I wanted other students that I tutor to feel reconnected with it while at home."

Like every excellent institution of higher education, it was clear to me that the college library is central to the Berkeley City College experience. Heather Dodge and Jenny Yap, librarians, were passionate and animated when talking about the school as an anchor institution for students, faculty, staff, and community.

Yap said, "It is not just the building; people make community happen . . . but our small campus building really does help create the community that exists here. . . . Some students stay the entire day. . . . It is a space where people want to be." Dodge jumped in, "Maybe it is because of all the glass walls, but I felt totally integrated into the [school's] community within a year. . . . Yes it can be a challenge, but I feel it is also a huge asset."

Both librarians told me how much they miss being in the building during the pandemic. "Everything is so open and connected in the building. There is a level of transparency and connection that I miss." Professor Linda McAllister added, "I love hanging over the rails and reaching out to a student who might have missed a class or an assignment." Dodge let me in on a college secret about the building: "There is a secret door that connects the college to the Y." "Don't worry," I said in a whisper. "I won't tell a soul."

While some talked fondly about the days when Berkeley City College was embedded in many sites within the community, and others talked about the "access, transparency, and community" of the one building at the center of the city, Professor McAllister told me that she and others are bringing some classes back out into the community. "Our department is taking some of our classes out into the community to increase the availability and access of students, and we are not the only department."

It seems to me that the pendulum of the college's history has settled in the best of all worlds—a campus at the center of the city, with departments providing classes out in the community at the sites that provide greater access for students. One of the benefits of a small college is the ability to make change swiftly. Making change to meet the needs of students and community is also indicative of the responsiveness of an anchor institution.

Berkeley City College serves a diverse mix of ethnic, cultural, and economic backgrounds. Like most community colleges, there are high school students, full-time workers, people who wish to transfer to a four-year university, and individuals who are the first in their families to attend college.

In 2019, the school enrolled 6,500 students per semester, of which 82% attended part-time and 18% full-time. About 26% of BCC students self-reported as Latinx, 23.9% Asian, 23.8% white, 15.5% African American, 7.4% as two or more ethnicities, 2.9% unknown, 0.3% Pacific Islander, and 0.2% as Native American. Eighty-two percent are between the ages of

19–24, 17% under 18, and 4.5% over 55. Eighty-nine percent are California residents, 8% international, and 3% out of state. Fifty-three percent identify as female and 44% as males. Berkeley City College offers 100 degrees and certificates, 23 career programs, and 11 degree programs with guaranteed transfers; and the lowest tuition rate per credit in the nation: $46.

The school maintains a strong collaboration with UC Berkeley. The college has the highest percent of transfers of any community college in the country and is second in the total number of students who transfer to UC Berkeley. It structures its transfer courses into guaranteed afternoon, evening, and Saturday schedules so that students can complete the UC and California State University (CSU) transfer requirements, even if they work full-time.

Also, with regard to its focus on transfer, The Campaign for College Opportunity recognized Berkeley City College 3 years in a row (2017–2019) as a "Champion for Higher Education" for the numbers of associate degrees for transfer awarded. Additionally, the college is being recognized as an "Equity Champion for Higher Education" for the number of associate degrees for transfer to Latinx students.

In my call with the Academic Senate, Heather told me about the importance of the California Master Plan in the mission and purpose of the school. "I don't think you can get a good picture of [Berkeley City College] without also understanding the California Master plan."

The California Master Plan for Higher Education establishes basic state policies on higher education. The original Master Plan was developed by a group convened by UC and the State Department of Education, as requested by an Assembly Concurrent Resolution in 1959. The Master Plan was completed in 1960.

The legislature has periodically authorized reviews of the plan that included recommendations for statutory changes. Major reviews were completed in 1973, 1987, and 2002. In 2010, a joint legislative committee on the Master Plan held a series of hearings examining higher education at the 50th anniversary of the plan.

According to the California Legislative Analyst's Office for Higher Education, the Master Plan does the following:

- *Assigns missions to the different higher education segments.* The Master Plan directs the California Community Colleges (CCC) to offer lower-division instruction that is transferable to four-year colleges, provide remedial and vocational training,and grant associate degrees and certificates. The University of California (UC) is to serve as the state's primary public research university and grant baccalaureate, master's, doctoral, and other professional degrees. The California State University (CSU) is to focus on instruction in the liberal arts and sciences and grant baccalaureate and master's degrees. (However, recent legislation has permitted CSU to offer doctorates under limited circumstances.)

- *Specifies eligibility targets.* According to Master Plan goals, the top 12.5% of all graduating public high school students are eligible for admission to UC, the top 33.3% are eligible for admission to CSU, and all persons 18 years or older who can "benefit from instruction" are eligible to attend CCC.
- *Expresses other goals for higher education.* The Master Plan includes a number of other statements concerning the state's higher education goals and policies. For example, it expresses the state's intent that higher education remains accessible, affordable, high-quality, and accountable.

The original 1960 Master Plan retains considerable authority as an expression of the state's higher education goals. However, additional state goals and policies for higher education are expressed elsewhere—such as in subsequent reviews of the Master Plan and in statute. For these reasons, the Master Plan can be thought of more as the major higher education policy goals embraced by the state, rather than a single written document.

With regard to the impact of that Master Plan on BCC and its community, Professor McAllister pointed to her students, "I have a wide range of students from a wide range of SES (socioeconomic status) . . . I have a student who lives in a storage shed because he has no home, and I also have students who might have gone right into the University but came to BCC because the academics were as good at a quarter of the cost . . . our students reflect the full range of the economic status of the community we serve."

When talking about the many partners BCC has in the community, Linda spoke about the departmental advisory boards that community members volunteer for. "They are vested in the college for sure, but they are also invested in the future of the community." So too, the faculty, staff, and (new) leadership of the college.

In spite of, and maybe because of, all that has changed and challenged BCC over the years, the faculty, staff, and leadership of the college have created a very special institution that does as it says it wants to—be transformative for students. BCC opens the doors to higher education for all in a community overshadowed by a major university that admits only the few. I left Berkeley thinking that the friction of the past has created a gem of a community college—an anchor of democracy excited about its future.

Reflections

First lady, Jill Biden has often been quoted as saying, "Community colleges are America's best kept secret." Berkeley City College (BCC) is a perfect example. Located within walking distance from the highly selective University of California, Berkeley (UC Berkeley), BCC has the highest transfer rate to UC Berkeley in the California Community College System. Situated between the university and Berkeley High School, BCC's central relationship to the community is unparalleled.

The COVID-19 pandemic highlighted the importance of BCC to its surrounding communities. As the college moved to remote learning, local businesses were negatively impacted by the loss of students, faculty, and staff who frequented downtown Berkeley establishments. At the time of this writing, the campus was still closed, and classes were held online. Still, the college found it important to send the message that the college was operating from a *physical* distance, but they are not *socially* distant. This distinction is critical for students' sense of belonging: to remind them they are a part of the college community even when they are not physically on campus.

The campus food pantry has played an increasingly important role as the campus moved to remote learning and operations. To ensure that all students have access to food when they need it, Berkeley City College partnered with the local food bank, Berkeley Food Network. This partnership allowed the campus to provide food to students while the campus was closed due to the COVID pandemic.

The pandemic, however, is not the only challenge that has faced Berkeley City College over the years. When it was founded in 1974, it was known as Vista Community College and was a "college without walls." Before moving into their current building in downtown Berkeley, the college had a variety of locations throughout the more northern parts of Alameda County. By 1977, the college had sites in more than 20 locations in response to the needs of local businesses and community organizations. By 1981, BCC maintained more than 200 sites—a difficult task for even the most skilled administrators. When their budget was reduced in 1987, the college was forced to reduce its offerings, transfer some programs to other colleges, and close some of its local sites. Previously serving mostly adult learners returning for job skills, BCC transitioned to a more comprehensive community college. The college's relationship and responsibilities to the community, however, did not change.

Currently, the college has a new president, Angélica Garcia, who joined a campus that was closed due to remote learning and operations. She therefore had to wait to meet many of her staff in person. Still, she wasted no time in demonstrating her priorities. As a first-generation college student and a woman of color, President Garcia recognizes the importance of putting students first. When she was announced as the school's next president, she talked about education as an "act of liberation" (Orenstein, 2020, para. 3), particularly for students of color.

Despite being in her 1st year at the college, President Garcia's commitment to the community is clear and unwavering. She has been energized by the racial, ethnic, cultural, and socioeconomic diversity of the community in which Berkeley City College is located. She talked about how the college is a "diamond, a pathway to liberation" that plays an important role in the lives of their students, their families, and their communities. She went on to explain how the campus provides social capital for students by being an anchor in the community.

An anchor institution is an urban institution that is considered fixed within a particular neighborhood or community (Ehlenz, 2018). While the infrastructure does not move, the college has demonstrated that in a remote environment BCC maintains its identity as an anchor in the city of Berkeley and Alameda County. As librarian Jenny Yap pointed out, the building is important, but it is the people who build community. In fact, some academic departments are moving their classes outside of the central campus building and going back out into the community. This was not a response to COVID-19; rather, it was a response to community needs. As one faculty member noted, being committed to the college means to be committed to the community.

Part of the commitment is to recognize the students who come to the college door bring assets with them, rather than deficits. Students shared how faculty and staff showed they were valued members of the Berkeley City College community. They talked about it being a place for dreams and second chances. Students also expressed their hopes of transferring to UC Berkeley, noting Berkeley City College's success on this measure.

Students also discussed the affordability of the college. This is particularly important because of California's Master Plan. In essence, the California Master Plan, established in 1960, was America's first "percent plan" as it attached percentages to the students who would be eligible for different sectors of California's public higher education system, including UC (9), CSU (23), and 116 community colleges. Although the UC and CSU institutions targeted enrollment rates of 12.5% and 33%, respectively, UC institutions only enrolled 10% of public high school graduates, and CSU only enrolled 18%, leaving more than 57% to enroll in a community college in 2018 (Kurlaender et al., 2018). While some universities enroll even lower percentages of eligible students, transfer is especially important at Berkeley City College. This is particularly the case as students of color and low-income students are more likely to enroll in two-year colleges than four-year. This great diversity is evident at the college, and the faculty, staff, and its new president are prepared to serve them.

Discussion Questions

1. What does it mean to be an anchor institution?
2. How important is it for community colleges to accept all who arrive at their door?
3. What responsibility do community colleges have for transferring students to four-year institutions? How can they best prepare students for transfer?
4. What does it mean to take an assets-based approach to serving students, particularly those who are racially, ethnically, culturally, and socioeconomically diverse? How do you do it?

10

CONCLUSIONS AND
RECOMMENDATIONS

*The greatness of America lies not in being more enlightened than any
other nation, but rather in her ability to repair her faults.*

—Alexis de Tocqueville

emocracy can never be realized until all people have equal opportunity to that increasingly elusive American Dream. As important as public schools have been toward those ends, 12 years is no
longer enough time to learn the skills and obtain the knowledge necessary
to achieve the dream. A college degree is now a requirement for most jobs
with family-sustaining wages. Economic and social mobility are not guaranteed as a result, but it is almost impossible without it. The wider the
door to opportunity the stronger the foundations of democracy. No segment of higher education has opened its doors wider to first-generation students, students of color, students of low-income backgrounds, place-bound
students, student parents, and immigrants—all who aspire to breathe free—
more so than community colleges. And no segment of higher education is
more significantly tied to the economic and social well-being of the communities they serve than the community colleges of America.

Community colleges are essential partners in the economic development
of the communities they serve and the preparation of their needed workforce. These colleges, for example, prepare a community's first responders
such as registered nurses, paramedics, EMTs, firefighters, and police officers. Community colleges have also become the institutions of choice for
incumbent workers upgrading their skills and displaced workers looking to
start anew. That work is especially important in a post-pandemic economy.
Community colleges develop curricula to respond to the needs of students
in the community as well as local economies, working closely with industry,

government, and other education sectors. It is the comprehensive mission of the community colleges that allows them to serve individuals, communities, and regions.

Community colleges respond quickly to meet community needs. Bob's experiences as a community college president and his campus visits give us stories of community colleges lending staff, students, and resources to hospitals, schools, and businesses long before and during the COVID-19 pandemic. Those stories and colleges are some of America's best examples of colleges at the social center of a community, innovative and agile in meeting social, economic, and workplace needs. Democracy and the sustainability of our nation are dependent on the strength and success of the communities we live and work in. Community colleges provide value and service to both individuals and communities.

We believe that there is an inexorable link between education, community, and democracy. We argue that education must be a key stakeholder toward that end, and community colleges play a critical role to meet that mandate. Indeed, the community colleges we highlighted in this book, like so many across the country, earned the mantle of "the community's college," the "people's college" as they maintain a commitment to open-door admissions. President Truman's 1947 Commission on Higher Education, as well as the development of Joliet Junior College, set the footprint and laid that foundation. Bob's experiences as college president and his in-person and virtual visits to five different community colleges across the country demonstrate that these campuses are building on that foundation.

Each college highlighted in this book represents different geographic regions and institutional sizes (from more than 2,000 students to more than 14,000). Most importantly, each campus also highlights different foci that establish these unique institutions as anchors of democracy in their various communities, whether rural or urban. It is important to note that several of the colleges we highlight now offer baccalaureate degrees and may or may not have *community* in their institutional names. Still, community is always present, and the members of their communities, on and off campus, recognize the significance of their college's mission to serve their respective regions.

Indeed, at the center of these institutions are dedicated and passionate faculty, staff, and administrators whose collective leadership serves to advance social and economic justice. Alongside them are racially, ethnically, culturally, linguistically, and economically diverse college students. Community college students face challenges and successes as returning veterans, adult learners, and students deemed academically underprepared.

The students we met wanted careers with livable wages as a result of their education. In response, these community colleges developed programs for transfer in partnership with four-year colleges and programs geared to the local workforce, partnering with local businesses. Equity, inclusion, and diversity were evident cultural values, embedded in their day-to-day functions. We found that the college communities had a keen understanding of and passionate commitment to the link between opening the doors of higher education and the sustainability of democracy.

We also noted that the community college faculty and staff we met recognized the importance of belonging and community to student success. In the AACC (1988) publication, "Building Communities: A Vision for a New Century," the authors define the term *community* "not only as a region to be served, but also as a climate to be created" (p. 7). These college leaders, faculty, and staff knew *why* and understood *how* to build and sustain a climate of community on campus. Student life centers, for instance, are often a space for community building, but the institutions in this book demonstrated that so too are fitness centers, college libraries, dining halls, outdoor learning labs, rodeo arenas, tutoring centers, as well as art, music, and academic learning studios. College leaders walked across their campuses with purpose, design, and authenticity, building community throughout the college. Education is, in the final analysis, a very human endeavor, and the people we met at these colleges understand that. The students certainly spoke passionately about community and belonging, suggesting it was significant to their college experience. Each of the colleges we presented in this book model the community their students, faculty, and staff want the world to become.

Community college leaders are clearly at the forefront in this endeavor as they are as active and engaged walking the halls of the community as they are walking the halls on campus. The presidents we talked with were fully engaged in the social and economic development of the communities they serve. "Yes" is the default response to a request for community collaboration. They sit on local boards and committees, working directly with local businesses, health care, and elected leaders on community challenges. Each seeks to attend every community celebration that time allows, and even when time does not. The leaders we talked with open their college's doors to significant community conversations as well as community activities. They are approachable, often engaging with members of the community while shopping in the local markets and attending community events. Each of the college leaders is visible and active in the betterment of community as a matter of practice, not just of theory.

Throughout this book, we celebrated the ways that community colleges have served as the "democratic arm" of higher education. Critical reflections, however, call upon community college leaders and those who care about these institutions to also be mindful of the challenges that continue to confront community colleges in their democratic missions. If this sector of higher education is to be successful, it must provide not just an open door; it must engage in an "honest assessment of, and genuine reckoning with, the structural barriers and hidden biases that pervade our own colleges and organizations" (Pasquerella, 2020, p. xvi). Only then will the community college sector make good on its promises of equitable opportunity and outcomes. To aid in that effort, we offer the following recommendations.

Community college leaders and practitioners must work to improve transfer and graduation rates, particularly since most students who walk through the doors of a community college aspire to earn a baccalaureate degree. While nearly half of all who graduate with a four-year degree once attended a community college, far too many students who enroll in a two-year institution never earn a degree or take far too long to do so, leading to real and opportunity costs.

Some institutions have sought to respond to these demands and concerns by offering their own bachelor's degrees, though outcomes, particularly for students of color and other students who have been underserved by more traditional four-year colleges and universities, are still unclear (Floyd & Skolnik, 2019). Indeed, more bachelor's degree completion data from these institutions are necessary. Meanwhile, community colleges offering only associate degrees must also seek innovative ways to support students to transfer and subsequently complete a baccalaureate degree. Further, institutions must maintain affordability by helping students to earn a credential and/or degree in less time.

This means that community colleges must also resolve the inequities within developmental education, particularly since many states have deemed them as the primary sector in higher education to offer such coursework. More specifically, community college practitioners have placed students in developmental courses at a higher rate than those at four-year institutions. While some would argue that students at community colleges are less prepared than those who enroll in four-year colleges, the data do not support that when it comes to developmental education enrollment, particularly as it pertains to the overrepresentation of Black and Brown student placement in developmental education courses. While some community colleges have accepted this challenge by revising the curriculum and supporting students more holistically with wraparound services, more institutions must see it as their responsibility to ensure that students placed into developmental education are placed appropriately and that students will complete required developmental courses and succeed in so-called college-level courses.

Indeed, the road to our democracy travels not only through federal or state government, but also through community college curricula, training, and services. Community college students often work, live, and attend college in the same community where they will likely stay, raise families, pay taxes, and engage civically. The community on and off campus must therefore be safe. The significant role community colleges play in educating and training first responders and police officers, therefore, cannot be overlooked. On the contrary, given the persistent racial violence and killings of Black and Brown men and women at the hands of police officers—most of whom were trained at community colleges—goals, practices, and values embedded within law enforcement training and education programs at two-year institutions must be a high priority and demonstrated commitment. Some community college and university systems have already begun doing this work. Minnesota state college leadership, for instance, has required incorporating antiracism education into their law enforcement and criminal justice curricula and has committed to hiring more racially diverse officers. For community colleges to continue to earn their reputation of being the community's colleges, more institutions must recognize they are, in part, responsible for the criminal behavior of some police officers, following campus training.

Throughout the book, and particularly in chapter 4, we've argued that leadership matters and a college's commitment to strengthen its efforts toward those ends takes more than a speech or two from the president. The sustainability of that work must emanate from top leadership, reinforced and driven by the mission statement and long-term strategic planning and built on a foundation of the necessary resources. The college's board of trustees must therefore be purposeful in the selection, development, evaluation, and compensation of its president to ensure that that president's values and vision are a fit with the college's institutional mission, culture, and commitments. College faculty buy-in is also essential. The selection, development and evaluation, and compensation of faculty and staff must also reflect the college's commitment to students and community alike. It is imperative that community colleges ramp up all efforts to increase the hiring of a more racially, ethnically, and gender inclusive and diverse leadership, faculty, and staff to better reflect the demographics of the student body and the community served. Indeed, community is developed and sustained from the inside out. We are clear, serving the community at large is not sustainable without first developing an inclusive environment of belonging and engagement on campus.

Community college leaders and practitioners, however, cannot meet these objectives alone as they are part of a larger system of higher education. And within that system, community colleges are woefully underfunded.

Their students and the communities they serve are being short-changed, increasing barriers to achievement and success in reaching their goals. That disjuncture between aspiration and opportunity further weakens our democracy. Eighty percent of the population deserve the same opportunities, resources, and investments as those available to the top 20% of our nation.

From 1980 to the publishing of this book, there has been a steady decline in state and federal support for community college funding. It was also during that period that community colleges saw increases in the number of students of color and students from low-income backgrounds. The steady decline of financial support over those 40 years alongside the steady increase in the numbers of students of low-income backgrounds and students of color raises questions related to racial equity and justice. At the same time, community college enrollment has been on the decline for the past several years. While enrollment for students of color seemed to remain relatively flat before the pandemic, we now see steep declines at community colleges with some suggesting for-profit colleges are the enrollment beneficiaries. If public two-year institutions are to remain the community's colleges, states will need to find ways to reinvest in them.

Indeed, a greater investment in college access, creating equitable outcomes, and stronger community-based partnerships between colleges and universities, health-care systems, nonprofit service organizations, business and industry, local government, and faith-based organizations should be high priorities of federal, state, and local governments. These investments will collectively strengthen and sustain communities. One size will not fit all. Shrink-wrapping ideas and plans to local communities is essential to the success of that local collaborative. The strength and sustainability of our democracy is dependent on it. Going forward, the funding and support for our public community colleges will be a key indicator of the course of racial justice, our democracy, and the degree in which we can "repair our faults."

We, as a nation of educators, business leaders, and policymakers, must view the rebuilding of America as an opportune time to make systemic change. We need to address both the symptoms and the causes of the viruses of racism and poverty that plague us, as community colleges, despite their open-access admissions policies, are not immune to these pandemics. Community colleges run the risk of becoming engines of inequity that further threaten our democracy without stable and committed leadership and if policies, practices, and curricula remain stagnant, if degree completion and success are not addressed, and if community colleges remain woefully underfunded. Opening the door to mediocrity not only diverts a student's achievement of a dream, but also escalates America's educational, social, and financial disparities. Our nation's experiment in democracy is teetering on the edge, and this moment will determine if it falls.

We hope the readers of this book, as graduate students, new and future leaders of community colleges, and policymakers, will consider their own roles in building our democracy. With that in mind, we end with some final questions:

1. If there were no community colleges, institutions with a commitment to open admissions and service to community, what would happen to the students they serve? The communities? States? A multiracial democracy?
2. What ideas or concepts in this book did you find most compelling to implement within your own spheres of influence? What recommendations would you make (and to whom) to create change?
3. What are some of the most important challenges facing community colleges today? How should they be addressed and by whom?
4. Who else in your academic and/or larger community should read this book and/or consider these questions?
5. What does your state leadership need to better understand about the impact of your college in your community? Who should be telling that story?

REFERENCES

Adams-Prassl, A., Boneva, T., Golin, M., & Rauh, C. (2021). *The Covid Inequality Project: Real-time survey evidence.* https://fedcommunities.org/wp-content/uploads/2021/08/covid-inequality-project-real-time-survey-evidence-crauh-08032021.pdf

African American Policy Forum. (2021). *Welcome to the #truthbetold campaign.* https://www.aapf.org/truthbetold

American Association of Colleges and Universities. (2021). *More than half of college students facing food and housing or food insecurity during the pandemic.* https://www.aacu.org/aacu-news/newsletter/more-half-college-students-facing-housing-or-food-insecurity-during-pandemic

American Association of Colleges and Universities News. (2017). *Food and housing insecurities disproportionately hurt black, first generation, and community college students.* Facts and Figures. https://www.aacu.org/aacu-news/newsletter/facts-figures/jan-feb2017

American Association of Community Colleges. (1988). *Building communities: A vision for a new century* (A report of the Commission on the Future of Community Colleges). Author.

American Association of Community Colleges. (2018). *AACC competencies for community college leaders* (3rd ed.). Author.

American Association of Community Colleges. (2019). *Community college enrollment crisis? Historical trends in community college enrollment.* https://www.aacc.nche.edu/wp-content/uploads/2019/08/Crisis-in-Enrollment-2019.pdf

American Association of Community Colleges. (2021). *AACC fast facts 2021.* https://www.aacc.nche.edu/wp-content/uploads/2021/03/AACC_2021_FastFacts.pdf

American Council on Education. (2019, November 18). Let's talk about race: An interview with Sylvia Hurtado. *Higher Education Today.* https://www.higheredtoday.org/2019/11/18/lets-talk-race-interview-sylvia-hurtado/

American Indian College Fund. (2011). *The first tribal college—Diné College.* https://collegefund.org/blog/the-first-tribal-college-dine-college/

American Institutes for Research. (2020). *The lasting benefits and strong returns of early college high schools.* https://www.air.org/news/press-release/lasting-benefits-and-strong-returns-early-college-high-schools

Anderson, N., & Douglas-Gabriel, D. (2021, March 4). Community colleges at a crossroads: Enrollment is plummeting, but political clout is growing. *The Washington Post.* https://www.washingtonpost.com/local/education/community-colleges-biden-covid/2021/03/01/7b30a18e-75df-11eb-9537-496158cc5fd9_story.html

Andrews, K. (2020, August 9). *CBS Sunday Morning*. https://www.cbsnews.com/news/this-week-on-sunday-morning-august-9-2020/

Artis, L., & Bartel, S. (2021). Filling the leadership pipeline: A qualitative study examining leadership development practices and challenges facing community college presidents in Illinois. *Community College Journal of Research and Practice*, *45*(9), 674–686. https://doi.org/10.1080/10668926.2020.1771476

Arviso, M. (2020). *The impact of Navajo Community College (now Diné College) on local communities* [Unpublished doctoral dissertation]. Fielding Graduate University.

Ashford, E. (2020). Community colleges on the front line. *Community College Daily*. American Association of Community Colleges.

Attewell, P., Lavin, D., Domina, T., & Levey, T. (2006). New evidence on college remediation. *The Journal of Higher Education*, *77*(5), 886–924. https://doi.org/10.1080/00221546.2006.11778948

Bailey, T., Jenkins, D., and Leinbach, T. (2005, September 28). *Graduation rates, student goals, and measuring community college effectiveness*. CCRC Brief, Community College Research Center, Columbia University. https://files.eric.ed.gov/fulltext/ED489098.pdf

Bear, A., & Skorton, D. (2018). *The integration of the humanities and the arts with sciences, engineering, and medicine in higher education: Branches from the same tree*. National Academies Press.

Belfield, C., & Jenkins, D. (2014). *Community college economics for policymakers: The one big fact and the one big myth* (Working Paper 67). Community College Research Center. https://ccrc.tc.columbia.edu/publications/community-college-economics-for-policymakers.html

Bell, D. (2004). *Silent covenants: Brown v. Board of Education and the unfulfilled hopes for racial reform*. Oxford University Press.

Benson, L., Harkavy, I., & Puckett, J. (2000). An implementation revolution as a strategy for fulfilling the democratic promise of university-community partnerships: Penn-West Philadelphia as an experiment in progress. *Non-Profit and Voluntary Sector Quarterly*, *29*(1), 24–45. https://journals.sagepub.com/doi/pdf/10.1177/0899764000291003

Benson, L., Harkavy, I., & Puckett, J. (2007). *Dewey's dream*. Temple University Press.

Benson, L., Harkavy, I., Puckett, J., Hartley, M., Hodges, R., Johnston, F., & Weeks, J. (2017). *Knowledge for social change: Bacon, Dewey, and the revolutionary transformation of research universities in the twenty-first century*. Temple University Press.

Bennet-Begaye, J. (2018). Look who's laughing now; The 50 years of Diné College. *Canku Ota*, *16*(10). http://turtletrack.org/IssueHistory/Issues18/CO1018/CO_1018_DineCollege.htm

Berkeley City College. (2021). *LGBTQIA home*. https://www.berkeleycitycollege.edu/LGBTQIA/

Billy, C. (2019). Pathfinders: Women leaders in the tribal college movement. *Tribal College: Journal of American Indian Higher Education*. *30*(4). https://

tribalcollegejournal.org/the-pathfinders-women-leaders-in-the-the-tribal-college-movement/

Blanco Ramirez, G. (2013). The global dimension of quality assurance in higher education. *International Journal of Technology and Educational Marketing (IJTEM)*, *3*(1), 15–27. http://doi.org/10.4018/ijtem.2013010102

Brint, S., & Karabel, J. (1989a). The community college and democratic ideals. *Community College Review, 17*(2), 9–19.

Brint, S., & Karabel, J. (1989b). *The diverted dream: Community colleges and the promise of educational opportunity.* Oxford University Press.

Brooks, D. (2019, February 18). A nation of weavers. *The New York Times.* https://www.nytimes.com/2019/01/17/opinion/learning-emotion-education.html

Burke, L. H., Jr. (2013). Why we can't wait: Diversity planning in community colleges. *Community College Journal of Research and Practice, 37*(11), 839–843. https://doi.org/10.1080/10668921003744934

Bynner, W. (1972). *The way of life according to Lao Tzu.* Perigee Books.

Carlock, M. (1986, March 30). From an unused building to a $100 million budget. *The Boston Globe.*

Case, A., & Deaton, A. (2015, December). Rising morbidity and mortality in midlife among white non-Hispanic Americans in the 21st century. *Proceedings of the National Academy of Sciences, 112*(49), 15073–15083. https://doi.org/10.1073/pnas.1518393112

Catallozzi, L. A. (2019). *How faculty beliefs shape teaching practice: A critical race collaborative action research approach toward achieving equity outcomes in community college remedial English* [Doctoral dissertation, University of Massachusetts Boston].

Center for the Analysis of Postsecondary Readiness. (n.d.). *Developmental education FAQs.* https://postsecondaryreadiness.org/developmental-education-faqs/

The Chronicle of Higher Education. (2017–2018). *The almanac of higher education.* Author.

Community College Research Center. (2020). *Community college FAQs.* Teacher's College, Columbia University. https://ccrc.tc.columbia.edu/Community-College-FAQs.html

Connors State College. (2019). Connors State College and Northeastern State University partner on nursing program. *Connections, 9*(5), 3–4. https://issuu.com/connorsstate/docs/connection_v9_i5

Connors State College. (2021). *Message from the president.* https://connorsstate.edu/president/

Conway, K. M. (2010). Educational aspirations in an urban community college: Differences between immigrant and native student groups. *Community College Review, 37*(3), 209–242. https://doi.org/10.1177/0091552109354626

Council for Higher Education Accreditation. (2019). *CHEA at a glance.* https://www.chea.org/sites/default/files/pdf/CHEA-At-A-Glance_0.pdf

Cremin, L. A. (Ed.). (1957). *The republic and the school: Horace Mann on the education of free men.* Teachers College Press.

Cromartie, J. (2018). *Rural America at a glance.* U.S. Department of Agriculture, Economic Information Bulletin. https://www.ers.usda.gov/webdocs/publications/100089/eib-221.pdf?v=1512

Cutolo, D., & Kenney, M. (2020, November 29). Platform-dependent entrepreneurs: Power asymmetries, risks, and strategies in the platform economy. *Academy of Management Perspectives, 35*(4). https://doi.org/10.5465/amp.2019.0103

Davis, R. (2019, January 25). Forty-two years serving up real life stories. *The Greenfield Recorder.* https://www.recorder.com/In-which-Richie-covers-his-own-speech-about-his-own-career-22998146

Dewey, J. (1902, October). The school as social center. *The Elementary School Teacher, 3*(2), 73–86. https://doi.org/10.1086/453152

Dickinson, E. (1964). *Final harvest: Poems.* Little Brown and Company.

Diné College. (2018). *Assurance argument.* https://warriorweb.dinecollege.edu/ICS/icsfs/mm/dinecollege_assuranceargument2018.pdf?target=ce11ecc3-88ec-4ee8-bc5f-c92c397d0bee

Diné College. (2020a). *Educational philosophy.* https://www.dinecollege.edu/about_dc/educational-philosophy/

Diné College. (2020b). *Who we are.* https://www.dinecollege.edu/about_dc/about-dc/

Diné College. (2021). *Institutional planning and reporting.* https://www.dinecollege.edu/about_dc/institutional-planning-and-reporting/

Douglass, F. (1845). *Narrative of the life of Frederick Douglass.* Anti-Slavery Office.

Dowd, A. C. (2003). From access to outcome equity: Revitalizing the democratic mission of the community college. *The ANNALS of the American Academy of Political and Social Science, 586*(1), 92–119.

Dowd, A. C. (2016). From access to outcome equity: Revitalizing the democratic mission of the community college. *The ANNALS of the American Academy of Political and Social Science, 586*(1), 92–119. https://doi.org/10.1177/0095399702250214

Dowd, A. C., Sawatzky, M., & Korn, R. (2011). Theoretical foundations and a research agenda to validate measures of intercultural effort. *The Review of Higher Education, 35*(1), 17–44. https://doi.org/10.1353/rhe.2011.0033

Dowd, A. C., & Shieh, L. T. (2013). Community college financing: Equity, efficiency, and accountability. *The NEA almanac of higher education,* 37–65. http://ftp.arizonaea.org/assets/docs/2013_Almanac_Dowd.pdf

Eddy, P. L. (2005). Framing the role of leader: How community college presidents construct their leadership. *Community College Journal of Research and Practice, 29*(9–10), 705–727. https://doi.org/10.1080/10668920591006557

Ehlenz, M. M. (2018). Defining university anchor institution strategies: Comparing theory to practice. *Planning Theory & Practice, 19*(1), 74–92. https://doi.org/10.1080/14649357.2017.1406980

Escalera-Kelley, L. N. (2020). *Puentes: Culturally sustaining learning environments in public, Hispanic-serving community colleges: Bridging cultural wealth, epistemic values, and pedagogical stances* [Doctoral dissertation, University of Massachusetts Boston].

Fain, P. (2019, May 30). College enrollment declines continue. *Inside Higher Ed.* https://www.insidehighered.com/quicktakes/2019/05/30/college-enrollment-declines-continue

Floyd, D. L., & Skolnik, M. L. (2019). The community college baccalaureate movement. In T. O'Banion (Ed.), *13 ideas that are transforming the community college world* (pp. 103–126). Rowman & Littlefield.

Frey, W. H. (2018). *Diversity explosion: How new racial demographics are remaking America.* Brookings Institution Press.

Frey, W. H. (2021, January 11). *What the 2020 Census will reveal about America: Stagnating growth, an aging population, and youthful diversity.* Brookings. https://www.brookings.edu/research/what-the-2020-census-will-reveal-about-america-stagnating-growth-an-aging-population-and-youthful-diversity/

Gawande, A. (2007). *Better.* Henry Holt and Company.

Gensler. (n.d.). *About.* https://www.gensler.com/about

Goldrick-Rab, S., Coca, V., Kienzl, G., Welton, C. R., Dahl, S., & Magnelia, S. (2020). *#RealCollege during the pandemic: New evidence on basic needs insecurity and student well-being.* Hope Center for College, Community, and Justice.

Gopalan, M., & Brady, S. T. (2020). College students' sense of belonging: A national perspective. *Educational Researcher 49*(2), 1–4. https://doi.org/10.3102/0013189X19897622

Grand Rapids Community College. (n.d.). *Promise Zone FAQs.* https://www.grcc.edu/grcc-promise-zone-scholarship/frequently-asked-questions

Grand Rapids Community College. (2018, October 30). *GRCC announces B. Afeni McNeely Cobham as chief equity and inclusion officer* [Press release]. https://www.grcc.edu/about-grcc/news/grcc-announces-b-afeni-mcneely-cobham-chief-equity-inclusion-officer

Grand Rapids Community College. (2019, December 10). *GRCC receives 3rd Impact Award in 5 years from West Michigan Works!* https://www.grcc.edu/communications/press/grccreceives3rdimpactawardin5yearsfromwestmichiganworks

Grand Rapids Community College. (2022). *Letter from the president.* https://www.grcc.edu/faculty-staff/institutional-research-planning/strategic-planning/strategic-plan-20182022#Letter%20from%20the%20President

Grand Rapids Community College TV. (2020, November). *GRCC equity report.*

Greenberg, M. (1997). *The GI Bill: The law that changed America.* Lickle.

Greenfield Community College. (2019). *The math studio.* https://www.gcc.mass.edu/math/studio/

Griffin, R. A., Ward, L., & Phillips, A. R. (2014). Still flies in buttermilk: Black male faculty, critical race theory, and composite counter storytelling. *International Journal of Qualitative Studies in Education, 27*(10), 1354–1375. https://doi.org/10.1080/09518398.2013.840403

Hardeen, G. (2006, February 23). Navajo Nation bids farewell to preeminent educator, Dr. Robert Roessel Jr., first Diné college president. *Navajo-Hopi Observer.*

https://www.nhonews.com/news/2006/feb/23/navajo-nation-bids-farewell-to-preeminent-educato/

Harper, S. R., Patton, L. D., & Wooden, O. S. (2009). Access and equity for African American students in higher education: A critical race historical analysis of policy efforts. *The Journal of Higher Education, 80*(4), 389–414.

Harvard University Faculty of Arts and Sciences. (2007). *Report of the Task Force on General Education.*

Haskie, M., & Shreve, B. (2018, August 20). Remembering Diné College: Origin stories of America's first tribal college. *Tribal College: Journal of American Indian Higher Education, 30*(1). https://tribalcollegejournal.org/remembering-dine-college-origin-stories-of-americas-first-tribal-college/

Healy, J. (2019, November 5). Farm country feeds America: But just try buying groceries there. *The New York Times.* https://www.nytimes.com/2019/11/05/us/rural-farm-market.html

hooks, b. (1994). *Teaching to transgress: Education as the practice of freedom.* Routledge.

Hostos Community College. (n.d.). *CUNY EDGE.* https://www.hostos.cuny.edu/Administrative-Offices/SDEM/CUNY-EDGE

The Institute for College Access and Success. (2019, August). *Dire disparities: Patterns of racially inequitable funding and student success in public postsecondary education.* https://ticas.org/wp-content/uploads/2019/09/dire-disparities.pdf

Jacobs, J., & Worth, J. (2019, March). *The evolving mission of workforce development in the community college* (CCRC Working Paper No. 107). https://ccrc.tc.columbia.edu/media/k2/attachments/EvolvingMissionWorkforceDevelopment.pdf

Jaschik, S., & Lederman, J. (2021). 2021 survey of college and university presidents. *Inside Higher Ed.* https://www.insidehighered.com/booklet/2021-survey-college-and-university-presidents

Johnson, L. B. (1964, January 8). *State of the union address.* https://www.presidency.ucsb.edu/documents/annual-message-the-congress-the-state-the-union-25

Kenney, M., & Zysman, J. (2016). The rise of the platform economy. *Issues in Science and Technology, 32*(3), 61. https://issues.org/rise-platform-economy-big-data-work/

Koh, J., Katsinas, S. G., & Bray, N. J. (2019). State financing for public community colleges: A comparative study of fiscal capacity and tax effort. *Journal of Education Finance, 45,* 198–216.

Kotkin, J. (2015, January 15). The cities where African Americans are doing the best economically. *Forbes.* https://www.forbes.com/sites/joelkotkin/2015/01/15/the-cities-where-african-americans-are-doing-the-best-economically/?sh=3ab7e7f5164f

Krishnamurti, J. (1964). *Think on these things* (J. Rajagopal, Ed.). HarperOne.

Kurlaender, M., Reed, S., Cohen, K., Naven, M., Martorell, P., & Carrell, S. (2018). *Where California high school students attend college.* Policy Analysis for California Education. https://edpolicyinca.org/publications/where-california-high-school-students-attend-college

Kurtinitis, S. (2019). Lifting every student. *Community College Daily*. American Association of Community Colleges.

Lazarus, E. (2018, August 13). The new colossus. *Encyclopedia Americana* (Vol. 10, p. 637). https://www.encyclopedia.com/people/literature-and-arts/american-literature-biographies/emma-lazarus

Least Heat-Moon, W. (1999). *Blue highways: A journey into America*. Little, Brown and Company.

Marroquín, C. (2019). *Tribal colleges and universities: A testament of resilience and nation building*. https://www.academia.edu/38975594/Tribal_Colleges_and_Universities_A_Testament of Resilience_and_Nation_Building

McClenney, K. M. (2007). Research update: The community college survey of student engagement. *Community College Review, 35*(2), 137–146. https://doi.org/10.1177/0091552107306583

McGuinness, A. (2014). *Community college systems across the 50 States*. National Center for Higher Education Management Systems (NCHEMS).

McNutt, K. S. (2018, July 29). Second chance Pell grants changing prisoners' lives. *The Oklahoman*. https://oklahoman.com/article/5602877/second-chance-pell-grants-changing-prisoners-lives

Merriam-Webster. (n.d.). *Binary*. Merriam-Webster.com dictionary. https://www.merriam-webster.com/dictionary/binary

Merton, R. (1951). *Social theory and social structure*. The Free Press.

Miller, M. T., & Kissinger, D. B. (2007). Connecting rural community colleges to their communities. In P. L. Eddy & J. P. Murray (Eds.), *Rural community colleges: Teaching, learning, and leading in the Heartland* (New Directions for Community Colleges, no. 137, pp. 27–34). Jossey-Bass. https://doi.org/10.1002/cc.267

Murakami, K. (2020, October 29). Racial equity in funding for higher education. *Inside Higher Ed*. https://www.insidehighered.com/news/2020/10/29/racial-disparities-higher-education-funding-could-widen-during-economic-downturn

Museus, S. D., & Harris, F. (2010). Success among college students of color: How institutional culture matters. In T. E. Dancy (Ed.), *Managing diversity:(Re)visioning equity on college campuses* (pp. 25–44). Peter Lang.

Myran, G., & Parsons, M. H. (2013). Overview: The future of the urban community college. In G. Myran, C. L. Ivery, M. H. Parsons, & C. Kinsley (Eds.), *The future of the urban community college: Shaping the pathways to a multiracial democracy* (New Directions for Community Colleges, no. 162, pp. 7–18). Jossey-Bass. https://doi.org/10.1002/cc.20054

National Association of Student Financial Aid Administrators. (2010). *NASFAA summary of the Higher Education Opportunity Act*. http://www.nasfaa.org/publications/2008/HEASummary.html

National Center for Education Data System. (2019). *IPEDS survey components*. https://nces.ed.gov/ipeds/use-the-data/survey-components/9/graduation-rates

National Center for Education Statistics. (2010). *Digest of education statistics, 2009*. U.S. Department of Education.

National Commission on Community Colleges. (2008). *Winning the skills race and strengthening America's middle class: An action agenda for community colleges.* The College Board.

The National Student Campaign Against Hunger and Homelessness. (2016). *Hunger on campus: The challenge of food insecurity for college students.* http://studentsagainsthunger.org/wp-content/uploads/2016/10/Hunger_On_Campus.pdf

National Student Clearinghouse Research Center. (2021). *COVID-19: Stay informed with the latest enrollment information.* https://nscresearchcenter.org/stay-informed/

Newell, M. A. (2014). What's a degree got to do with it? The civic engagement of associate's and bachelor's degree holders. *Journal of Higher Education Outreach and Engagement, 18*(2), 67–90. https://files.eric.ed.gov/fulltext/EJ1029882.pdf

New England Commission of Higher Education. (2021). *Standards for accreditation.* https://www.neche.org/resources/standards-for-accreditation

NPR News. (2014, January 8). *For LBJ the war on poverty was personal.* https://www.wbur.org/npr/260572389/for-lbj-the-war-on-poverty-was-personal

Obama, B. (2008, February 6). *Super Tuesday speech* [Video]. YouTube. https://www.youtube.com/watch?v=8dzHDzvTfzQ

Obama, M. (2018). *Becoming.* Crown.

Orellana, D. A. (2019). *Organizational culture in community colleges: Making connections to diverse student success* [Doctoral dissertation, University of Massachusetts Boston].

Orenstein, N. (2020, April 7). *Berkeley City College names Angélica Garcia as new president.* Berkeleyside. https://www.berkeleyside.org/2020/04/07/berkeley-city-college-names-angelica-garcia-as-new-president

Palmer, P. (1998). *The courage to teach.* Jossey-Bass.

Parker, T. L. (2012). *The role of minority-serving institutions in redefining and improving developmental education.* Southern Education Foundation.

Pasquerella, L. (2020). Foreword. In T. McNair, E. Bensimon, & L. Malcolm-Piqueux (Eds.), *From equity talk to equity walk: Expanding practitioner knowledge for racial justice in higher education* (pp. xv–xvi). Wiley.

Postsecondary National Policy Institute. (2020). *Fact sheets: Native American students in higher education.* https://pnpi.org/native-american-students/

President's Commission on Higher Education. (1947). *Higher education for American democracy: A report of the President's Commission on Higher Education.* U.S. Government Printing Office.

Pura, R. (2016, June 22). Dickens, film, and beyond duality. *Greenfield Recorder.* https://www.recorder.com/Dickens-film-and-beyond-duality-2792756

Putnam, R. (2015). *Our kids: The American Dream in crisis.* Simon & Schuster.

Rendón, L. I. (2002). Community college puente: A validating model of education. *Educational Policy, 16*(4), 642–667. https://doi.org/10.1177/0895904802016004010

Reuben, J. L., & Perkins, L. (2007). Introduction: Commemorating the sixtieth anniversary of the President Commission's report. *History of Education Quarterly, 47*(3), 265–276. https://doi.org/10.1111/j.1748-5959.2007.00100.x

Rhoads, R., & Valadez, J. (1996). *Democracy, multiculturalism, and the community college*. Routledge.

Roberts, M. T. (2020). Racism in remediation: How Black students navigate stereotypes to achieve success in developmental mathematics. *Community College Journal of Research and Practice, 44*(10–12), 701–721. https://doi.org/10.1080/10668926.2019.1640143

Rural Community College Alliance. (2021). *About*. https://ruralccalliance.org/about/

Rydberg, J., & Terrill, W. (2010). The effect of higher education on police behavior. *Police Quarterly, 13*(1), 92–120. https://doi.org/10.1177/1098611109357325

Schein, E. H. (1985). *Organizational culture and leadership: A dynamic view*. Jossey-Bass.

Schults, C. (2001). *The critical impact of impending retirements on community college leadership*. American Association of Community Colleges.

Schultz, P. (1984). *Deep within the ravine*. Viking.

Senge, P. (1990). *The fifth discipline: The art and practice of the learning organization*. Doubleday/Currency.

Shah, M. (2021). *Analysis of loss of work during the COVID-19 pandemic in the United States*. Georgia State University. https://scholarworks.gsu.edu/iph_capstone/129

Shapiro, D., Dundar, A., Huie, F., Wakhungu, P. K., Yuan, X., Nathan, A., & Hwang, Y. (2017). *Tracking transfer: Measures of effectiveness in helping community college students to complete bachelor's degrees* (Signature Report No. 13). National Student Clearinghouse Research Center.

Solomon, J. (2018, January 15). MLK Day at GCC: Continuing that train of people coming together. *Greenfield Recorder*.

Soto, H. (2018). *Implementation of a civic engagement community change model by a community college through the integration of technology and social media as strategic element* [Unpublished manuscript].

Tachine, A., Cabrera, N., & Yellow Bird, E. (2017). Home away from home: Native American Students' sense of belonging during their first year in college. *The Journal of Higher Education, 88*(5), 785–807. https://doi.org/10.1080/00221546.2016.1257322

Teranishi, R., Suárez-Orozco, C., & Suárez-Orozco, M. (2011). Immigrants in community colleges. *The Future of Children, 21*(1), 153–169. https://www.jstor.org/stable/41229015

Thoreau, H. D. (1961). *Cape Cod*. Thomas E. Crowell.

Torpey, E. (2020). *Education level and projected openings, 2019–2029*. Bureau of Labor Statistics. https://www.bls.gov/careeroutlook/2020/article/mobile/education-level-and-openings.htm

Two Bears, D. (2014). *The Navajo reservation, the Navajo people, and social mobility: The American Mosaic; the American Indian experience*. ABC-CLIO.

Urban, C. (2019, March 24). Senior Symposia planned at Greenfield Community College's downtown center. *The Republican*. https://www.masslive.com/living/2013/01/senior_symposia_planned_at_greenfield_community_colleges_downtown_center.html

Warren, C. (2017, November 21). The gentrification of the urban community college. *Inside Higher Ed*. https://www.insidehighered.com/views/2017/11/21/community-colleges-should-stay-true-their-core-essay

Wells, R., Manly, C., Kommers, S., & Kimball, E. (2020). Narrowed gaps and persistent challenges: Examining rural-nonrural disparities in postsecondary outcomes over time. *American Journal of Education, 126*(1), 1–31. https://doi.org/10.1086/705498

Wheatley, M. (2002). *Turning to one another*. Berrett-Koehler.

Wheatley, M. (2006). *Leadership and the new science*. Berrett-Koehler.

Whistle, W. (2020, April 17). College graduates are less likely to become unemployed due to the coronavirus. *Forbes*. https://www.forbes.com/sites/wesleywhistle/2020/04/17/college-graduates-are-less-likely-to-become-unemployed-due-to-the-coronavirus/?sh=42aab0af61e4

Wilson, R. (2017, June 27). Changing America: America's growing education divide. *The Hill*. https://thehill.com/homenews/campaign/339585-changing-america-part-vi-americas-growing-education-divide

Wilson, K. B., & Cox-Brand, E. (2012). Reading the competencies through a feminist lens. In P. L. Eddy (Ed.), *Leading for the future: Alignment of AACC competencies with practice* (New Directions for Community Colleges, no. 159, pp. 73–83). Jossey-Bass. https://doi.org/10.1002/cc.20028

Wood, L. J., Harris, F., III, & Delgado, N. R. (2017). *Struggling to survive: Striving to succeed*. Community College Equity Assessment Lab. https://www.lumina-foundation.org/files/resources/food-and-housing-report.pdf

Zook, G. F. (1947). *Higher education for American democracy: A report of the president's commission on higher education* (Vols. I–VI). Harper & Brothers.

ABOUT THE AUTHORS

Robert L. Pura retired after 40 years of service as a teacher and administrator in the Massachusetts Community College System, the last 18 as president of Greenfield Community College. Bob is a proud graduate of Miami Dade Community College where he earned his AA degree. He then went on to earn his BA at the University of South Florida, MS from St. Thomas University, Miami, and PhD from The University of Texas at Austin.

Pura served on the New England Commission on Higher Education and the Commission for Academic, Student, and Community Development for the American Association of Community Colleges, was a member of the Working Group on Assessment of Student Learning for the Massachusetts Department of Higher Education, and chaired the Massachusetts Community Colleges' President's Council. Pura also served on the boards of the American Association of Colleges & Universities, Bay State Health Systems of Western Massachusetts, the Community Foundation of Western Massachusetts, The Food Bank of Western Massachusetts, the Franklin County Chamber of Commerce, and the International Language Institute.

Pura is currently senior fellow for community college leadership at the University of Massachusetts Boston's College of Education and Human Development.

Tara L. Parker is chair of the Leadership in Education Department and professor of higher education at the University of Massachusetts Boston. Her research focuses on race and higher education, including three interrelated areas: (a) the application of critical race theory to higher education; (b) the experiences and contributions of faculty of color; and (c) the influence of public policy on developmental education and its implications for college access and success.

Parker's scholarship has been published in the *Review of Higher Education*, *Teachers College Record*, the *Journal of College Student Development*, and the *Community College Journal of Research and Practice*. She has presented her work in Canada, China, Mexico, Thailand, and throughout the United States. Parker is the author of *The State of Developmental Education: Higher Education and Public Policy Priorities* (Palgrave MacMillan, 2014) with Leticia

Bustillos and Michelle Sterk Barrett and *Racism and Racial Equity in Higher Education* (Jossey-Bass, 2015) with Samuel Museus and Maria Ledesma.

Parker was awarded the 2020 Presidential Medal Honorable Mention at the Association for the Study of Higher Education (ASHE) for her influence as a local change agent. She currently serves on the editorial board for *Review of Higher Education* and the *American Educational Research Journal.*

Prior to joining the faculty at the University of Massachusetts Boston, Parker earned her PhD from New York University, her MA from the University of Minnesota, and her BA from Marist College.

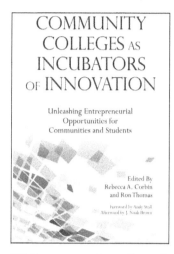

Community Colleges as Incubators of Innovation

Unleashing Entrepreneurial Opportunities for Communities and Students

Edited by Rebecca A. Corbin and Ron Thomas

Foreword by Andy Stoll

Afterword by J. Noah Brown

While community colleges have traditionally focused on providing students with opportunities to gain credentials for employment, the increasingly important question is: Are they preparing students for the looming dynamic, disruptive, and entrepreneurial environments ahead?

This book addresses the urgent need for community colleges to prioritize entrepreneurship education both to remain relevant in a changing economy and to give graduate students the flexible and interdisciplinary mindsets needed for the future of society. It argues that entrepreneurial education should be offered broadly to a wide range of students, and across all disciplines; defines the key constructs for achieving this objective; and describes how to create entrepreneurial learning environments.

"Entrepreneurial thinking has the power to facilitate transformational change within our colleges, and this book captures the essence of not only how it can, but why it should. Whether energizing educators to seek innovative curriculum designs, or creating partnerships to better address complex workforce issues in the 21st century, the contributing authors make it clear that the entrepreneurial college is the new standard of excellence."
—*Edwin Massey, President, Indian River State College*

Leadership Theory and the Community College

Applying Theory to Practice

Carlos Nevarez, J. Luke Wood, and Rose Penrose

Foreword by Eduardo J. Padrón

"Nevarez, Wood, and Penrose have struck the right chord with *Leadership Theory and the Community College*. This text offers an innovative approach to case analysis that encourages the reader to engage in reflective practice. The authors effectively align theoretical perspectives and the application of leadership principles in steering deliberation on problems and solutions. This work is a definitive compendium of community college case studies that will provide a useful framework for emerging and current community college leaders."
—*Eboni M. Zamani-Gallaher, Professor and Coordinator, Community College Leadership Program, Eastern Michigan University*

This book presents leaders and aspiring leaders in community colleges with a theoretical and practical framework for analyzing their leadership styles, and determining the dimensions of leadership they need to improve in order to strengthen their capacity to resolve complex issues and effectively guide their institutions.

It does so through presenting theories about leadership that are congruent with the notions of equity, access, diversity, ethics, critical inquiry, transformational change, and social justice that drive the missions of community colleges, and at the same time provides the reader with the strategic skills to prepare for and navigate the profound changes ahead.

Undergraduate Research at Community Colleges

Equity, Discovery, and Innovation

Nancy H. Hensel

Foreword by Gail O. Mellow

This book aims to highlight the exciting work of two-year colleges to prepare students for their future careers through engagement in undergraduate research. It emerged from work in five community college systems thanks to two National Science Foundation grants the Council for Undergraduate Research received to support community colleges' efforts to establish undergraduate research programs. Chapters 1, 2, and 3 provide background information about community colleges, undergraduate research, and the systems the author worked with: California, City University of New York, Maricopa Community College District (Arizona), Oklahoma, and Tennessee. Chapter 4 examines success strategies. The next five chapters look at five approaches to undergraduate research: basic/applied, course-based, community-based, interdisciplinary, and partnership research. Chapters 10, 11, and 12 discuss ways to assess and evaluate undergraduate research experiences, inclusive pedagogy, and ways to advance undergraduate research.

Today there are 942 public community colleges in the United States, providing affordable access to 6.8 million students who enrolled for credit in one of the public two-year institutions in the United States. Students are more prepared for the next step in their education or careers after participating in quality undergraduate research experiences.

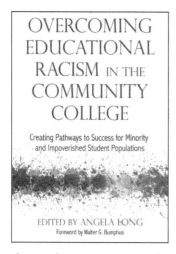

Overcoming Educational Racism in the Community College

Creating Pathways to Success for Minority and Impoverished Student Populations

Edited by Angela Long

Foreword by Walter G. Bumphus

"America's community colleges are well positioned to act, with urgency, to address the issues of racism that are inhibiting the academic progress and success of far too many students. *Overcoming Educational Racism in the Community College* uses evidence to point the way toward changes colleges can make—and must make—to end the structural inequities that keep students of color from completing their educational journeys ready to achieve their full potential. Angela Long's essential book shows colleges how to plan with equity in mind and act with equity in mind."—*Karen Stout*, *President, Achieving the Dream*

"What an incredible collection of research, best practices, and leaders on the most important topic of our nation—how to address inequity caused by educational racism. Community colleges are uniquely positioned to provide the opportunity for consciousness and job skills for those most underserved. As was the aim of the Obama administration, improving the graduation rates from community colleges—where the majority of first-generation, African American, Latino, Native American and working-class students attend—is the only way to educate our Nation and be, once again, the most educated country."—*Jose A. Rico*, *Former Executive Director, White House Initiative on Educational Excellence for Hispanics*

"Community colleges are one of the great economic engines of America and this groundbreaking new book by Angela Long highlights the importance of community colleges as they operate with rapidly changing demographics, funding headwinds, and requirements for increased social impact. Educational equity requires inclusion for all Americans and this textbook traverses all the racial and ethnic mosaic of what makes America great including a rational portrayal of the Asian and Pacific Islander American diaspora and the AANAPISI campuses who support them."—*Neil Horikoshi*, *President and Executive Director, Asian and Pacific Islander American Scholarship Fund*

The American Association of Colleges and Universities

The American Association of Colleges and Universities (AAC&U) is a global membership organization dedicated to advancing the vitality and democratic purposes of undergraduate liberal education. Through our programs and events, publications and research, public advocacy and campus-based projects, AAC&U serves as a catalyst and facilitator for innovations that improve educational quality and equity and that support the success of all students. In addition to accredited public and private, two-year and four-year colleges and universities and state higher education systems and agencies throughout the United States, our membership includes degree-granting higher education institutions in more than twenty-five countries as well as other organizations and individuals. To learn more, visit www.aacu.org.